בס"ד

How to Excel in Learning

Techniques for Accelerating Your Progress in Learning Gemorah

by

Rabbi Yerachmiel Shlomo Basner

Translation of Section on

Hadracha* in Learning from *Emrei Chayil

How to Excel in Learning

Copyright 2002

Second Edition 2017

All rights reserved. No part of this publication may be copied, retrieved, or translated without express permission from the author.

Comments and requests for copies or for permission for reprints of this publication may be addressed to:

Rabbi Basner, 1 Mesilat Yosef, Kiryat Sefer,

Israel tel: 08-974-1696 afoykc@gmail.com

How to Excel in Learning

אלתר חנוך העניאך בלאאמו"ר הגרח"ד הכהן ליבאוויטש
RABBI A. HENACH LEIBOWITZ
67-18 GROTON STREET
FOREST HILLS, N.Y. 11375

Rabbinical Seminary of America
Dean

ראש הישיבה
ישיבת רבנו ישראל מאיר הכהן
בעל "חפץ חיים" זצ"ל

כ"ב אלול תשנ"ט

הנני בזה להמליץ בעד התלמיד היקר הרב ירחמיאל בסנר שליט"א שלמד בישיבתנו
בארה"ב ובארץ ישראל.

ידוע ומפורסם שבדור האחרון זכינו לראות פעולות נשגבות עם בעלי תשובה שבאו
להסתופף בצילה דהמנותא מתוך אמונה ואהבה אמיתית לאביהם שבשמים.

ומח מאוד שמחתי לשמוע שתלמידי היקר רחש לבו לדבר טוב לארגן וליסד ישיבה כזה
לחוזרי בתשובה שבשם "ישמח לב" יכונה.

ישיבה זו מיועדת ללמוד תורה בדרך ישראל סבא כפי מסורתנו הקדושה מתוכננת
להבנת כל יחיד ויחיד.

ועד נוסף לזה להחשיש לוח להחריש בלבם עקרי חדת ע"י לימוד המוסר וההשקפה ע"פ באורי חכמנו
זכרונם לברכה.

הרב בסנר הוא בעל מדות נעלה וגדול כחו להשפיע ולהדריך דור חדש של תלמידים
המבקשים והצמאים לשמוע דבר ה'.

מה מאוד נחוץ בדורנו אנו לחזק ידי אלו העוסקים בזה שהם באמת "שלוחי דרחמנא
ושלוחי דידן".

הנני לסיים בברכה ובתפילה לקל בורא עולם שיזכה להרבות כבוד שמים בפעולותיו
ושנזכה כלנו יחד במהרה לביאת אליהו ולקיום של "יהשיב לב אבות על בנים ולב בנים
על אבותם".

הכו"ח לכבוד התורה ועמלי,
מוקירו,

3

How to Excel in Learning

בית מדרש עליון לתורה "יד אהרן"
High Academy of Torah "YAD AHARON"
מיסוד המוסד התורני על שם אהרן ורחל חיות ירושלים.
Founded by the Aharon & Rachel Chajuss Torah Foundation, Jerusalem.

Established by
Hagaon Harav
Bezalel zolty זצ"ל
Chief Rabbi of Jerusalem

Yeshiva

Kollel

Talmudic Library

Free Loan Fund

Scholarship Fund

Student Aid Fund

How to Excel in Learning

בס"ד

משה מרדכי קארף
קרית ספר

תאריך:

How to Excel in Learning

הרב מאיר גפני
רב בית הכנסת המרכזי "היכל יצחק".
רח' חפץ חיים 6 מודיעין עילית.

תאריך: כו טבת תשע"ד.

הסכמה

הנה הרה"ג רבי ירחמיאל שלמה בסנר שליט"א ראש הכולל ישמח לב וישיבת כתר חיים בעיה"ק ירושלים ופה בעירנו מודיעין עילית. העלה בקולמוסו חידושי תורה נפלאים בסוגיות הש"ס. ובנוסף כתב מאמרים נפלאים בהדרכה לתלמידים בדרכי הלימוד ורבה התועלת המופקת ממאמרים אלו למחנכים ולתלמידים. ובנוסף צירף מאמרי הסברה לסוגיות בש"ס הבנויות על חשבון לתועלת הלומדים. וכל זאת ערך בכשרון רב ובטוב טעם. ויהי רצון שיעלו דברי תורתו על שולחן מלכים ויזכה להמשיך בפעולותיו הברוכות לזיכוי הרבים.

הכותב לכבוד התורה ולומדיה

מאיר גפני.

Except from HaRav Meir Gafne`s approbation:

...In addition, he has written insightful pointers for guiding talmidim

in the craft of learning and much benefit can be derived from it

by mechanchim as well as talmidim.

Besides this, he has included numerous sections on sugyos which are interwoven with the field of mathematics...

How to Excel in Learning

Table of Contents

7 Table of Contents
9 Acknowledgments
12 Introduction
14 Middos
19 Goals of Learning in Yeshiva
24 The Derech Halemud in Yeshivas Chofetz Chaim
32 Depth and Breadth
53 Importance of Analyzing Each Word
55 Levels of Understanding
58 Recognizing the Logic Used in Learning
64 Both are the Words of the Living G-d
69 The Text and the Commentaries
73 Preliminaries for Learning
75 Learning with a Chavrusa
77 Choosing a Chavrusa
78 Preparation for the Shiur
80 Taking Notes
90 Participation During the Shiur
92 Criticism
95 Disagreeing with the Rebbi
96 Review of the Shiur
98 Use of Recorders
101 Remembering by Heart
102 Use of Time

How to Excel in Learning

103 Using Tutors to Your Best Advantage
104 Listening to Lectures
105 Originating Chidushim
106 Delivering a Chabura
108 How to Teach According to this Derech
115 Asking a Posek
117 Glossary
122 Table of Contents of Emrei Chayil
151 About the Author

How to Excel in Learning

Acknowledgments

Although in the introduction to my sefer *Emrei Chayil* I have expressed my gratitude to many, I feel compelled to mention here specifically the help that my son, Reb Moshe, and my daughter, Mrs. Tehillah Hoffman extended to this work by editing the Hebrew version of it Moshe, from his perspective of having learned in Israeli yeshivos, challenged and provided feedback to what I had written, forcing me to clarify a number of very important points. My daughter spent many hours editing the Hebrew edition. She patiently delt with my almost constant revisions to this guide, and certainly with the larger, major work of *Emrei Chayil*, which required her to reread dozens of times the same text, often containing only minute changes. As a result of their efforts, the original Hebrew version became expanded and enriched. These new additions were then incorporated into the English version. The language and style has been improved over the original, and that is due to my daughter's gift of expression.

I also must mention my appreciation for my dear friend, colleague, and host for my stays in Chicago, Rabbi Yirmiyahu Spector, who took time from his busy schedule to look through and make numerous corrections in the English version.

Last, but not least, I am indebted to my wife for her assistance in the preparation of this work.

However, after all is said, I personally accept the responsibility of all mistakes that may be found in the language, as well as in the formatting. I say this because of my having made many changes after the editors had finished their work.

In case the reader feels that I should have had at least made some statement acknowledging the Yeshiva Chofetz Chaim, my answer is that specific references will be made to the Yeshiva and its Hanhalah in the text itself. Even the innovations that are mine were developed in a yeshiva that supported such efforts and this itself is a tribute to the Yeshiva.

Introduction

Let me suggest that the reader use one of the learning skills that our beloved Rosh HaYeshiva, Maran HaRav Alter Henoch Henach Leibowitz, *zt"l*, taught us, which was to first skim over the text before attempting to delve into its details. In this way the reader will see the entire framework of the ideas presented here. Afterwards, he can scrutinize each technique.

A successful *talmid* naturally receives positive appreciation from those in his surroundings and consequently feels self-satisfaction. One to whom success does not come so easily faces a serious challenge.

Over the years, a number of books have stressed the importance of positive reinforcement to students by their *Rebbeim* and parents. Since I feel, and I am certainly not alone, that the actual success itself outweighs all the positive reinforcements of Rebbeim, parents and peers, I have felt obligated to compile a guide about how to achieve that success. Many have spoken of the importance of providing *simcha* in learning for the talmidim in order to motivate them. A major significant source of simcha in learning comes when the *Yeshiva bochur* has actually successfully attained a new level of ability. This is the real achievement and gives the greatest genuine self-satisfaction to the student, spurring him onwards.

In the past, the *Gedolim* have expressed the desirability of integrating weaker students into the framework of mainstream Yeshivas. In order to implement such a strategy, it would be necessary to provide those students with specific tools to cope in such an environment. I believe that the techniques which I will be discussing can raise the level of weaker talmidim, possibly even transforming them into top-notch talmidim. Top-notch talmidim utilizing these techniques can attain even higher levels of their potential. The procedures focus one's natural abilities to tackle the art of learning. Many of the ideas are equally applicable to girls in seminary, or anyone taking courses in secular business subjects.

Needless to say, if you or your talmidim are doing well you may already be aware of whatever is written here. However, if this not the case, I urge you to first skim the entire guide and then to please read it over carefully. See if there are points which you have not previously incorporated in your learning.

Middos

"The beginning of wisdom is fear of Hashem"(*Tehillim* 111:10). The entire subject starts here. If we look at *Avos* (3:11), " Rebbi Chanina ben Dosa says, 'Whenever fear of sin precedes wisdom, that individual's wisdom will be lasting.'"

This means that one must start with basic *emunah* that the Creator gave us His Torah and that He wants us to learn it, and therefore He will help us learn it. The last point follows from the understanding that all abilities, and especially the ability to learn and understand the Torah, are *matanos*, gifts, from *HaKodesh Baruch Hu*.

Together with this, as with all endeavors, one needs *tefilah*.

We say at least three times a day in *Ashrei* "Hashem is close to all those who call upon Him truthfully." The implication is that in order for tefilah to be effective, one must be seeking the desired goal for its truthful purpose, namely as means of serving Hashem, and not for honor, wealth, or other reasons. The more someone exerts all his ability into his learning, the more he will actually feel what he is missing, and consequently, the more sincere will his desire be to attain greater levels of clarity in his learning. Therefore, one should *daven* for it with this feeling. HaRav Avroham Yellin, *zt"l*, writes in *Orech Hapanim* that one who davens for *ruchniyius* with tears will be answered.

Humility is essential for becoming and remaining a receptacle for Torah. Humility requires that one recognize that all his abilities, especially the ability to learn and to understand Torah, are gifts from HaKodesh Baruh Hu. Even after having achieved understanding, one should remain an *anav*, remembering that just like another talmid does not understand now, so too you did not understand it before you received the precious matana of understanding. (See *Sotah* 21b.)

How to Excel in Learning

Now the question remains, "what is the proper *hishtadlus*, the practical steps, needed for success in learning?"

Every step that is mentioned here needs patience. These are new skills to be learned and it may take time to internalize them.

We learn in *Avos* (2:6) "One who is bashful cannot learn." This rule is very important because if a student is embarrassed to ask questions because he does not want his peers and Rebbi to think that he does not understand, then with the passage of time it will become true, and will grow more and more truer. However, if he will vanquish his pride and not pay attention to his honor, then by asking, he will learn and know. Furthermore, if he becomes oblivious to his pride, he will eventually find that he will be able to present his novella to others and gracefully accept their criticism and sometimes even their disdainful laughter. This will only sharpen him and with time he will become a great *lomdan,* presenting *chidushim* that no one will be able criticize!

The Rosh HaYeshiva, *zt"l* in *Chidushei Haleiv* brings the Medrash (*Medrash Rabah* 8:3) on the *pasuk* (*Devarim* 30:11) "[The Torah] is not beyond you…" which states that the obligation on every individual to learn the entire Torah causes many to give up even before they begin, therefore one should remember the Mishnah in *Avos* (2:21) where Rabbi Tarfon says, "It is not upon you to complete [the learning of the Torah]." Nevertheless, even this obligation itself can bring one to great aspirations when combined with the quote "every single individual in the Nation of Israel must ask himself, 'When will my actions reach the level of those of my forefathers?'" He concludes "therefore, when one delivers *Mussar* to others, or even to oneself, one must be aware of their emotional state at that time to determine whether your words are likely to improve their conduct or cause to opposite and make them give up, become depressed and lax in their performance." We can see from his words that it is very important that the student learn how to encourage himself, for example, by focusing on his success, however minute it may seem to be. We already learned this particular approach from Rabbi Akiva`s conclusion upon seeing the drops falling on the stone.

Goals of Learning in Yeshiva

The policy of the Rosh HaYeshiva, *zt"l* was that the purpose of a Yeshiva was not merely to provide a place for students to open their *seforim* and learn, but rather that it should be a place where *bochurim* could be trained in the art of learning *Gemora* so that they would eventually become *Gadolim* in Torah, *Yirei Shimayim*, and *ba`alei middos Tovos*. I would like to emphasize that, although he constantly spoke with the assumption that the talmidim would play leadership roles when they left the Yeshiva, he never said that one of the purposes was to help make that bochur a Gadol Hador. It is my personal opinion that the reason for this distinction is that, in order to become a Gadol Hador, the individual must be endowed from HaKodesh Baruch Hu from a very early age with intellectual abilities beyond the realm of the rest of his generation. Nevertheless, one who is not so endowed but still accepts upon himself to become a giant in learning, may in the end actually attain becoming a Giant Leader of his generation also. However, there are two differences in these two goals. One who yearns to be the next leading sage of his generation, may in fact be motivated merely to attain honor. This is a problem because, as we mentioned before, humility is one of the essential components of success in learning. Furthermore, the desire to become the next Gadol Hador is liable to bring him on a path full of such overwhelming frustration that he will give up and may leave learning altogether. In contrast, the goal of becoming a lomdan will not bring him to so much frustration that will break him and force him to leave learning altogether, but rather will help him develop into someone who can stand up to the trials of living and to attain fulfillment all the days of his life. This is because the same intellect that he developed to learn Gemora and Mussar is what he naturally uses for conducting his own life. If he doesn`t, gentle feedback will suffice to put him on the correct track.

There are two major goals in learning. The first is to learn how to decipher the language of the Gemora. The second is to learn how to think with accurate, precise logic. Although a translation can be helpful, to accomplish these goals one needs a Rebbi who will learn with him with these goals in mind. *HaGaon*, HaRav Yisroel Salanter, *zt"l* writes in *Ohr Yisroel*, Letter 6,"The primary obligation on the young student is to acquire the capability of learning.... The learning of Torah, which is worthy of that name, is learning with sharp clarity, where each one clings to his own theory..." We see that he emphasizes the process of learning how to learn in depth. In Letter 27, he defines learning Torah in-depth, as "the ability to become an expert in Torah, to sharpen the intellect, to be fluent in it, to straighten his thinking, to the point that he can engage with others in the battles of Torah and uproot mountains with his *pilpul*."

The ability to learn develops in stages during the course of the student's life. For purposes of illustration, we will use the names of the levels according to the Israeli system. It begins, generally, while the student is in Yeshiva Ketana, (ages 13-17) where he is expected to acquire the skill of translating and understanding on a superficial level. Afterwards, in Yeshiva Gedolah, while he still is in a *shiur*, he is expected to research all the citations of whichever text he is asked to prepare, to read with the understanding of the logical flow, the

How to Excel in Learning

approach of the author, and the difficulties that the author is addressing and his answers, and the difficulties on what the author is presenting and how they can be answered. (It seems to me that it is a good idea to stay in one Rebbi`s shiur until the talmid is trained in the Rebbi`s approach and can come up with the inferences that the Rebbi makes on a regular basis. The talmid should still continue in that shiur until he has so many thoughts and calculations to make that he cannot handle both the Rebbi`s and his own.) Then he is ready for the next higher shiur or next stage whatever it maybe. Later, he joins the *kibbutz* and composes *chaburas* to present to his peers. His goal is to explain the words of Rishonim, Achronim and Roshei HaYeshiva. The next level is to strive to identify and understand the pivot points upon which these authors base their logical dilemmas when the authors have not expressed these points clearly. Then there is a level in which the talmid feels that there exists difficulties in the text and he toils on them until they become clear and subsequently, after additional effort, he thinks of solutions, often arriving at the words of the commentaries. Above this level is when he can ask critical questions on his own theories before others ask them. (In the Hebrew version we have brought the words of the Ramchal on this point.) All of what we have just presented is part of true toiling in learning. If one will go through all these steps in their proper order, then, B`ezras Hashem, he will feel fulfilled and taste the sweetness of learning Torah during each of these stages.

The Derech Halemud in Yeshivas Chofetz Chaim

Before I begin this topic I must clarify that the Rosh HaYeshiva, *zt"l*, did not see this guide. Everything that I am writing here and elsewhere about Yeshivas Chofetz Chaim is according to my own personal assessment based upon what I

How to Excel in Learning

observed and heard during eighteen years that I spent in the Chofetz Chaim system, partly based upon what the Rosh HaYeshiva, *zt"l*, said, partly from my Rebbeim, and partly from my fellow talmidim. Therefore, it is possible that some of the *B`nei HaYeshiva* will not agree with everything that I have written on this topic. Perhaps I have inadvertently neglected essential fundamentals. Nevertheless, according to my judgment, what I have written will be useful for the serious reader, either for himself or for his talmidim, therefore I did not refrain from presenting these ideas. For those readers who are not part of the Chofetz Chaim system, it may be helpful to be aware that some of the fruits of the derech are available in the sefer *Birkas Dovid*, which contains shiurim of the Rosh HaYeshiva, *zt"l*, and in *Chidushei Haleiv*, which contains his Mussar *Shmuzim*.

How to Excel in Learning

In order not to offend any single individual, I will begin by saying that there is no doubt that there are exceptional talmidim in every place, in every Yeshiva, and in every derech of learning. The goal of our words here is to answer the question, "Is there a way that I can improve upon my present level of learning?" It is also not my intention to suggest that there is only one answer to this question. It is possible to say that for every mind, there is a different derech in learning. What I did hear from the Rosh HaYeshiva, *zt"l*, was that all the Yeshivos in Europe, before World War II, learned the way that Yeshivas Chofetz Chaim was learning. This statement can be very startling for someone familiar with the numerous Yeshivos which existed then, each with their own derech. What I believe the Rosh HaYeshiva, *zt"l*, was referring to was the preliminary stages before each unique derech comes into play. That is, the initial logical steps which are necessary to build up each *sugya* before coming to the stage of answering the difficulties. The uniqueness became apparent in the answers. With regard to differences in questions, if one Rosh HaYeshiva failed to ask

the question that another asked, it doesn't mean that he held it was not a suitable question. It could be that he was busy enough with his own questions and felt they were sufficient to begin searching for answers. I would venture to say that only at this second stage of answering and explaining the sugya can we apply the Chazal,
"Both of these are the Words of the Living G-d."

The Derech of the Yeshiva can be found quite clearly spelled out in general terms by the Ramchal in *Derech Tevunos* Chapter 10. However, the specific questions which were constantly being heard within the walls of the Yeshiva are presented in *Darchei HaGemora*. For this reason I have added a specific section for this sefer in my larger work, *Emrei Chayil*.

In general, the Rambam's *Yad Hachazaka* was not learned in the Yeshiva. The reason I heard

How to Excel in Learning

was that the Rambam wrote the *P`sak Halacha* and not to explain the sugyos. Therefore, he wrote tersely and without giving reasons. In contrast, Tosefos and other Rishonim clearly ask questions and answer them in addition to stating their reasoning. The difference is that when one is learning Tosefos, one can test the accuracy of a theory against the text, seeing if each letter, word, and even order of the discussion matches the theory. The Derech of the Yeshiva teaches the talmid how to test his theory. This process of determining what exactly is being said is the *mitzva* of toiling in Torah and is what refines the *ruchnyios* of the talmid. To accomplish this with the Rambam, the very first step would be to know the entire *Yad Hachazaka* by heart. That would eliminate many talmidim from any of these benefits.

The Yeshiva also gave tremendous importance to the value of learning the Acharonim, to the point that every word and letter was weighed on a scale. This is because they knew Shas and

How to Excel in Learning

Poskim by heart, as well as in-depth. The Roshei HaYeshiva of pre-war Europe are included in this category.

There are an additional three points of the Derech of the Yeshiva that made an impression on me. The first is that the Rebbi of the shiur would provide the talmidim with a list of all the references to be discussed during the upcoming shiur, either the day before or at least in the morning before the shiur. Similarly, a list of all the material to be discussed would be publicized a few days before the Rosh HaYeshiva, *zt"l*, would present a pilpul shiur. The rationale is simple: the material is challenging enough even when the talmidim have seen them before the shiur.

The second point is the discussion-style of the shiur. The Rebbi would not lecture. He spent the time asking the talmidim probing questions. If they became stuck then he would lead them to progress. The goal was to train them to think, so there was no point just to give answers. Many of the Rebbim gave the talmidim the responsibility of leading the shiur, each taking a turn on a daily rotation. Whatever the format, the talmidm had the priority of asking and answering before the Rebbi. The Rebbi, together with the talmidim, would explore the pros and cons of both the questions and answers. He would guide them to see if what was being offered was consistent with the words of the text and if it was logical.

It is fitting to emphasis here that the Rebbi was careful to listen to the ideas with appropriate respect in order not to embarrass the talmid. The entire discussion was done with an air of both seriousness and joy of learning the true meaning of the Torah, even if there were times that the Rebbi could have dispelled the notions of the talmidim immediately. Only after the students finished asking their questions would the Rebbi ask his questions one by one, allowing for discussion after presenting each question. Similarly with the answers, the talmidim answered first. Only afterwards would the Rebbi present his approach.

The third point was that the talmidim were expected to review and know each day's shiur to the point that they would be able to say it over to the Rebbi. They were not necessarily separately tested each day, but due to the open discussion, it was obvious to the Rebbi who knew the material and who did not.

The next section also contains fundamental elements of the derech.

I would like to finish this part with an addition detail. I have never stated or written that what I presented in my shiurim or what I have written in my sefer conform to the derech of the Rosh HaYeshiva, *zt"l*, neither in their level, or in the choice of texts (aside from Rashi, Tosefos, and the Maharsha) or even in what the Rosh HaYeshiva, *zt"l*, may have felt I was capable of attaining. What I can say is that I believe that the time that I spent in Yeshivas Kesser Torah and Yeshivas Chofetz Chaim branches, both in New York and Yerushalayim, have profoundly influenced whatever I have learned, taught, and written. I leave it for others to decide as to whether or not they conform to the derech.

Depth and Breadth

In *Horayos* (14a), the Gemora asks, "What is preferable, to be a Sinai or an up rooter of mountains?" Looking from the outside it would appear that there are Yeshivos which lean to one of these sides and others which lean to the second side, and there really isn't any grave importance to this situation. However, as we enter more into the subject, we may conclude that perhaps there are profound consequences. It seems pretty clear that in this generation no one argues with the goal of attaining both

How to Excel in Learning

depth and breadth. In addition, no one argues that the talmid starting out needs a daily *seder* in *iyun*, as well as in *b`kiyus*. The question is only how much time should be allocated for each.

There is a major difference between the environment of a talmid learning in Eretz Yisroel and one learning in America. (Other countries fall into their appropriate place according to the criteria that follow.) In Eretz Yisroel, on one hand, they are surrounded, *bli ayin hara*, by great Rabbonim and *Talmidei Chachomin*, and many who are *B`kyim b`Shas*.

On the other hand, the talmidim generally stop learning all secular subjects at a rather early age. All their friends and family are in the same situation. Therefore, when they learn according to the norm, they are filled with simcha and satisfaction and nothing disturbs them. They feel this satisfaction when they cover ground in learning. One who completes many *dapim*, *pirakim*, and *mesechtos* can easily feel his progress. This is not the situation in America. There, the talmidim continue to learn secular subjects until they enter Yeshiva Gedolah. Some continue to learn these subjects in university. Even if they don't, they may have friends or family members that do. In university, some of the subjects depend upon exacting logic, and also the talmidim may meet many other students who are very gifted intellectually (I am not suggesting that everything that they say is correct, I merely mean that they are quick to grasp and to apply what they learn and originate their own theories). This being the case, how will a talmid, who cannot delve into the depth of the Talmud, feel when he is in their proximity? Where is this situation liable to go? It for this reason it is imperative for the American talmid to focus on in-depth learning. In contrast to what we mentioned above, one who spends a lot of time remaining on one page or even one line, even though he has, in this process, studied many Acharonim and thought through many *s`voros*, may find it hard to discern his progress until after a long period of many months. Only then does he feel that his capability has improved. So with regards to self-satisfaction, he has to develop patience. This type of derech would be very challenging to an Israeli due to his environment. The typical American Yeshiva, however, is set up for this. When I was learning in the Yeshiva, the new talmidim constantly received encouragement from the Rebbeim as well as from the older bochurim. What I have presented, from my small vantage point, is what I think the basis is for the difference in the prevailing opinions of the Gedolei Hador of Eretz Yisroel and America about how to run a Yeshiva for the general population.

How to Excel in Learning

There seems to be another area of differing opinions. At first glance, the above discussion finds its application in an ordinary student without a particular preference towards any specific direction, or if he has, it hasn't become clear to him what it is, or for someone starting an institution and has not yet decided what its framework will be. The Rosh HaYeshiva, *zt"l*, was concerned, besides seeing in his experience, that someone who is accustomed from an early age not to analyze what he reads, when he gets more mature, will still not be able to delve more than superficially, without the ability to reach even the simple explanation of the text. I imagine that this occurs because from the beginning he did not develop the patience to exert himself more than to spend the time for an initial reading. On the other hand I imagine, the Gedolim in Eretz Yisroel are concerned that one who spends time in iyun will find it difficult to learn b`kiyos at a fast enough pace to cover substantial breadth.

How to Excel in Learning

Another case is where the talmid stops learning, at any age, and as a result he never gets a chance to acquire the other part of learning. Which is better from the standpoint of developing his capabilities of learning, if he had learned iyun or b`kiyos?  With regard to learning, if he had already learned many dapim, he can continue in his derech and set aside time every day to learn b`kiyus. But the question is "Will he be able to create a strong bond to learning based on just superficial reading?" Another question is, "Will he be capable of raising his level of learning and to fulfill what Reb Yisroel Salanter, *zt"l* says?" In contrast, one who has spent his early years training in iyun, is always motivated to seek out b`kiyus. Those who feel that one must learn iyun at a set speed, cannot ask a question on the Rosh HaYeshiva, *zt"l*, because even the Rosh HaYeshiva, *zt"l* agreed that we need Yeshivos which do not learn according to his derech, because not every talmid is able to devote himself with the intensity and the patience required for this derech.

I would like to relate an incident which occurred to me which is on this topic. When I was just starting out to learn at Yeshivas Kesser Torah, my advisors, who were interested in my welfare, were concerned that the quota of learning there was very small. Because I had heard that many years previously, HaGaon Reb Yaakov Kamenetsky, *zt"l*, had sent his son to learn in Yeshiva Chofetz Chaim when HaGaon Harav Dovid Leibowitz, *zt"l*, was still alive, I thought that a simple solution to satisfy my friends would be to accompany my friends to Reb Yaakov, *zt"l* and ask him if I should change Yeshivas. Reb Yaakov, *zt"l*, answered that I should go to a Yeshiva that learns at a quicker pace. (The reader must understand that I was extremely happy learning where I was and I was putting all my effort into it. I also was not ready to learn any faster. If I had tried I probably would have lost everything. I say this on the basis that a few years later I learned with someone who was much faster than I was. I soon had to stop, because it is very frustrating to keep turning the daf, not knowing a tenth of what was being said.)   When I returned to the Yeshiva, the Rosh HaYeshiva, HaGaon Rabbi Elyakim Getzel Rosenblatt, *shlita*, explained that Reb Yaakov, *zt"l* answered the question as if there was a question. That is, he answered with the assumption that I was not happy in the Yeshiva where I was learning. From this incident I concluded that a *Posek* would not advise a bochur to continue to learn in a Yeshiva in which he is not happy, assuming that he has already honestly tried his upmost to be successful and that he has other choices to go to. He also would not advise a talmid to enter into a Yeshiva which is following, in the view of outsiders with whom the talmid must interact, a relatively extreme style of learning. He would only give such advice to a talmid who already expressed his deep commitment to such a derech. Maybe the Posek would also agree if he saw that the bochur had potential towards a certain derech, even if he was still rather young.

The question also arises when a talmid wants to put extra time into his learning. However, since he does not have a burning desire in any specific direction, he cannot decide for himself as to where he should devote his extra time and strength. Here too, no one would argue that he should go against his natural tendencies. For example, there could be a student who doesn't have the patience to stay focused on one point more than a short time. He needs time to develop this trait. For him, it is not worth spending the available time on iyun. It would only cause him frustration and waste his time without any benefit. On the other hand, for one who feels that the speed is too fast, a bigger

How to Excel in Learning

quota is liable to cause him to give up completely. Therefore, the first bachur is ready to give more time to b`kiyus, while the second bachur to iyun. Only after each one is ready, should he spend extra time to work in that area of his own weakness.

The style of learning can have significant influence on the talmid`s self-esteem. If we accept the results of a survey, 90% of males have stronger analytical minds and only 10% have stronger memory-oriented minds. If so, then suppose a talmid, who is part of the 90% group that doesn`t have a strong memory, whose self-esteem still depends on the praise and reactions of others, goes in the path of b`kiyus and even though he has learned many dapim, because his memory is weak, he cannot recall what he has learned. He will not receive too much praise or encouragement from his environment and he will be frustrated by his inability to remember what he has learned. If that is the case, how will he have a healthy self-esteem? However, if that same talmid would embark on a course of intense in-depth learning and he studies under a Rebbi who appreciates the benefits of learning with depth, who has a good self-esteem and is joyful with his life and his portion of Torah depth, then he will be able to influence this talmid and guide him to become an *amkan* and to develop a self-esteem which is independent of others. Then his self-esteem will be enhanced when he see that he has a high level of understanding of the Talmud and that his ideas are found in the writings of our illustrious ancestors. And even if he were to be successful in remembering his b`kiyus, what will become of his analytical capabilities? (We already mentioned how the Rosh HaYeshiva, *zt"l*, would have answered this question.) Understandably, those of the 10% who have the brocha of a fine memory would be successful if they chose the path which emphasizes breadth.

There are other fundamental differences between them. The Rosh HaYeshiva, *zt"l*, often quoted his father, HaGaon Reb Dovid, *zt"l*, as saying, "Everyone sees the greatness of the *baki*, but they don't see his shortcomings; on the other hand, everyone sees the weakness of the *amkan*, but they don't see his greatness." Then he explained, "Everyone sees the greatness of the *baki* because he is fluent in all of Shas, but they don't see his shortcomings, that is, the lack of understanding of what he has read, because they cannot delve sufficiently into all the numerous citations that he presents in his lectures to determine if what he says is actually plausible. On the other hand, everyone sees the weakness of the amkan, since they see that he is not aware of many Gemoras, *Halachos,* and concepts. Only a few recognize his greatness in the depth of understanding, because only a few are even close to his level to appreciate the difficulties that he presents and the solutions that he suggests.

An additional distinction is with regards to memory. If the baki fails to remember all that he learned, what is the advantage of having spent his time with superficial reading? In contrast, Harav HaGaon Rabbi Shmuel Niman, zt"l, said in the name of Reb Dovid, *zt"l*, that there was a talmid that had to leave the Yeshiva to earn a living. Years later, when he returned, he was able to regain his previously sophisticated level of depth within a relatively short time. B`ezras Hashem, the acquisition of skills of in-depth learning remains with the talmid throughout his entire life.

How to Excel in Learning

The Rosh HaYeshiva, *zt"l*, said that a Posek receives *Siyatta Dishmaya*, special D-vine Assistance, to arrive at the correct Halachic decisions. The implication is that it also applies for a Rav who is not on the highest level of learning and understanding. The reason they receive this extra assistance is in order that they can provide guidance for those who come to them. I would like to add to this idea and say that it would seem also to apply to a Rebbi, Magid Shiur, and a Darshan. That is, Hashem helps them in a way that they can help their audience. However, it does not necessarily mean that we should transcribe and study their words like those of an Acharon.

Despite this, he never said this referring to a baki, that even though he toils in learning Torah, that he would be assisted in arriving at the deepest insight. I am sure that there were many opportunities for him to mention this if he thought it to be true. If the amkan must toil with all his ability and still remains in doubt as

How to Excel in Learning

to the correctness of his conclusion, why would Hashem reward the one who doesn't even begin to exert himself in iyun?! At this point, let me relate what I witnessed when I was visiting one of the branches of the Yeshiva. Although I was not close enough to hear each word clearly, I believe that the conversation went as follows: A young student just starting out in the High School asked the Rosh HaYeshiva, *zt"l*, if he would he please give him a bracha to become a Talmid Chachom. The bracha of the Rosh HaYeshiva, *zt"l*, was: "You should merit to toil and exert yourself in learning Torah and reach the level of a Talmid Chachom." Then he explained to him, "But without toil and exertion, Hashem does not give us His gift of Torah."

With regards to character traits, the one who concentrates his efforts in gaining depth, even though he may often arrive at the conclusions of the Torah Giants of the earlier and later epochs, nevertheless, the chances are that he will remain with his humility because it is quite clear to him that there remains much for him to still learn, since he sees all the tractates and seforim that he has not even touched upon yet. When he realizes that the Maharsha, for example, wrote on all Shas, and makes a calculation as to how long it would take the talmid to understand all the Maharshas and then realizes that he did not even understand Tosefos before looking at the Maharsha, he will shudder in awe before the Maharsha and certainly will not put himself in his league. This is true even if he believes that he has a valid *kushiya* on the Maharsha, because he knows that he may be wrong and even if he is right, he doesn't know the rest of Shas to the depth that the Maharsha knows it. And even if he did complete Shas, he realizes that he did not do so on the deep level that even he himself is capable of reaching. He also knows that there are many in-depth seforim which he has not learned, besides those which he hasn't even heard of. Furthermore, he becomes more humble because he sees how weak he is in knowledge and wisdom. Perhaps the most important factor is that those insightful thoughts that he has come up with, he recognizes as gifts from Hashem, for he remembers that previously his mind was blank and only after much toil and labor, suddenly new clues occurred to him. After more toil, more ideas surfaced. So it is easy for him to view his superior insight as only a gift from Hashem. He will certainly treat his peers and talmidim the way he would have liked to be treated before he had understood the point. To end off, as was just mentioned, since, according to Reb Dovid, *zt"l*, this type of deep thinker does not receive honor from the general populace for his brilliance; his humility is not jeopardized from that sector.

How to Excel in Learning

I would like to return to an item mentioned earlier in passing. I heard the Rosh HaYeshiva, *zt"l* say at least once, "We (referring to the b`nei HaYeshiva of Chofetz Chaim) are all frustrated, because this derech is very frustrating." He said it seriously, but he said it cheerfully. If this is so, how are we expected to carry this burden? I would like to answer based on my own experience. To the degree of frustration, that is the degree of fulfillment. The more one exerts himself in trying to understand, so proportionately will his feeling of joy be when the topic finally does become clearer to him. When those on the bottom hear this message from the top they are more likely to accept it and wade it out. Another important item is the ability to appreciate each minute step as a precious gift from HaKodosh Baruch Hu. The third thing is to consider that the more effort that is put into the present sugya, the deeper the talmid`s understanding will be in the next sugya. Also, there was a built–in limit in the

How to Excel in Learning

Yeshiva as to how long the talmid had to endure any frustration. The talmid was expected to leave the Yeshiva in search of a position or to earn a livelihood after fourteen years of learning. This knowledge probably made it easier to bear any discomfort. (Of course many have chosen to continue to strive for higher levels of understanding, despite the incumbent frustration, even after having left the structured system of the Yeshiva. In fact, I would say, that when the derech is self-imposed by the talmid he is able to reach even higher levels than when he was under the jurisdiction of the Yeshiva. This I attribute to the fact that when he is on his own, whether he giving a shuir or learning by himself, he is now faced with a myriad of possibilities which previously his Rebbi dealt with, but which now he must sort through.) Finally, there was motivation to continue despite the disappointments, due to the character traits, *yiras Sh`mayim*, and depth of learning of the Rosh HaYeshiva, *zt"l*, and the

How to Excel in Learning

Rebbeim, *yb"l*, as well as of the more advanced talmidim, that was attributed to their mastering this derech in learning. But someone who is afraid of frustration, how can he ever elevate himself, even slightly, above his present level?

There is an additional point which will clarify what was said above, that it is not worth it to try to go against the natural traits of the talmid. As was hinted before, there is a great difference if some outsider, for example, the Rebbi, pushes the talmid against his nature or whether the talmid is pushing himself. If the talmid himself wants to become an amkan, and he is prepared to accept all the embarrassment and frustration, and to face numerous setbacks with no limit and to get up and return to the battle and not to swerve from the path until he gets to the target; then certainly it is proper for him to choose this derech. Chazal teach us, "Nothing stands in the way of commitment", "In the path

How to Excel in Learning

that a man wants to walk in, [Heaven sends messengers and] they escort him in it", and "One who comes to purify himself, [Heaven sends angels so that] they will assist him."

For those who feel that this derech prevents them from seeing much of Shas, there is a possible solution. A daily seder in learning Mishnayos, with brief commentaries, is one way to amass a broad knowledge of Torah *Sheba`al Peh*.

It is fitting to finish this section by relating that towards the end of his life, the Rosh HaYeshiva, zt"l, made a *siyum* on *Shas* in the Yeshiva. To my knowledge, his intention to make a siyum was not generally known until close to the time of the actual siyum. This was in accordance with his character, since all his life he covered up his greatness. If I understand correctly, it is because, although it was important for him to complete Shas, it was more of a priority for him to teach his talmidim how to learn. It seems that he did not publicize his intention to make the siyum not only due to his humility, but also because he did not want to intimidate the talmidim. The psychology is that to the extent that the talmidim feel that the Rebbi has vast knowledge and already knows the answer to a problem, to that degree they will not exert themselves to find an answer using their own abilities. However, by having the actual *siyum* in public in the end, he showed that learning in this derech does not preclude eventually finishing Shas.

Importance of Analyzing Each Word

One may ask, "How important is it to be able to understand and account for every word in the text, even of an Acharon?" The answer is based on the following. They were very precise in the choice of their words. Therefore, we must be precise in our reading of their words. The major task in learning is called critical analysis. This entails synchronizing and balancing an intepretation of the text with acceptable logic. *P`shat*, the simple meaning, must fit the language as well as be logical. All learning, as well as understanding any of the commentaries, hinges on this.

To think logically, a mind must be able to hold a train of thought containing numerous syllogisms. One way to train one's mind to do this is to repeat over the logic of others who are reputed to be very logical. This should be done until one's own mind becomes accustomed to doing it. Eventually, B`ezras Hashem, he will be able to do it by himself. This is all the more so with regard to understanding the depth contained in the Talmud. Therefore, the talmid who wants to elevate his level of thought, must listen and read, and then repeat over the thoughts of Talmidei Chachamin.

Levels of Understanding

1. Transitory- understanding while listening, but loss of it soon after the lecture is over. Similarly, understanding while reading, but forgetting quickly after the sefer is closed. These levels may mislead the talmid into feeling that he has good understanding.
2. Assisted recall- can reconstruct the lesson with the assistance of notes.
3. Unaided recall- can reconstruct the lesson without the assistance of notes.
4. Learned- ability to recall what was said even after an extended time interval.

The goal of learning is to understand what is said with clarity, and to retain this for unlimited time. Therefore the standard that one should accept upon oneself is that the definition of understanding is the ability to repeat over what was heard or read with comprehension.

How to Excel in Learning

As stated previously, we must progress step by step. If we start at the lowest degree we should not be discouraged, but rather strive to raise ourselves and, with Siyata D`shmaya, we will climb up level by level.

In order to grow one must make a *kinyun* on the shiur.

The ultimate goal of review is to be able to say over the shiur without looking at any notes.

The best way to review is to do it with the Rebbe, getting every point clearly. If you cannot make such an arrangement, try to get help from the top talmidim who know the shiur best. You may have to alternate between these talmidim so that you are not always taking the time of only one of them.

What happens if you cannot get help from the Rebbi every day and other talmidim do not give you the clarity you need? For this a recorder can serve a valuable role.

The ultimate goal is to transcribe every statement of the shiur. In this process you will be forced to determine the true meaning of every word and each sentence. Even if it seems to take too much time to determine the meaning of one word, it is worth it. Remember all the words that you understood during shiur and after the first listening to the recording you already understand. Hopefully, whatever was missed during the shiur and the first few sessions with the recording will be understood in subsequent sessions after having mastered more material of the shiur. The more you work using your own potential, the more you will sharpen it. Of course, you may reach a point where you feel that it will be quicker to ask your Rebbi.

Recognizing the Logic Used in Learning

There are two types of logical flow which must be mentioned, namely deductive (or a priori logic), and inductive (or a postori logic). Webster's New World Dictionary defines them as follows:

Deductive logic – reasoning from the general to the specific, or from a premise to a logically valid conclusion.

A priori – from cause to effect or from a generalization to particular instances; deductive.

Inductive logic – reasoning from particular facts or individual cases to a general conclusion.

a posteriori – from effect to cause, or from particular instances to a generalization; inductive.

Propositions – an informative statement whose truth or falsity can be evaluated by means of logic.

Premise a) a previous statement or assertion that serves as the basis for an argument, or b) either of the two propositions of a syllogism from which the conclusion is drawn

syllogism a) an argument or form of reasoning in which two statements or premises are made and a logical conclusion is drawn from them (Ex: All bar mitzvah boys are older than thirteen [major premise]; Sam is a bar mitzvah boy [minor premise]; therefore, Sam is older than thirteen [conclusion]), or b) reasoning from the general to the particular.

Hypothesis – an unproven proposition tentatively accepted to provide a basis for further argument.

Since inductive logic is investigatory, working backwards in an attempt to discover the fundamental rules, there can be numerous conclusions drawn. The *Tannah, Amorah, Rishon, Acharon*, or later Commentary either presents all his alternative conclusions or he selects the conclusion which he feels is best in the context of his broad knowledge of the entire Talmud. Each attempt to arrive at an inductive conclusion is a hypothesis. Each hypothesis must be checked by deductive logic and for its consistency with the rest of the text and the rest of the Talmud. Once we are aware of these steps we will be better equipped to recognize them when they occur in the Talmud and its commentaries. We can also begin using these tools ourselves. Generally, however, for the last step we must rely on the Rishonim and Acharonim, who knew the entire Talmud by heart.

The majority of the logic found in the Gemora is inductive. A case is presented and then it is followed by an attempt to figure out the rule upon which it is based. This is much more difficult than deductive logic in which a rule is given and then it merely has to be applied. Knowing this, we can understand why a student who previously did well in applying the rules he was given may suddenly become totally confused when he is first introduced to Gemora. Unfortunately he may remain confused until he clearly understands the difference between the two. If a Rishon is using inductive logic and the talmid thinks he is using deductive logic, the talmid at best, may admit that he does not understand. At worst, *Chas V`shalom*, he may lose faith in the exalted words of the Rishonim!

Now we must mention the most powerful tool in learning. As previously mentioned, the goal of learning is to determine *p`shat* in the text. This is done by the process of inventing a hypothesis and then testing for its logic and consistency with the text. Based on the results of this analysis we make adjustments to form a new hypothesis and then again test it. This is repeated until we have no reason for further corrections. What forces us to make adjustments are *kushiyas*. A kushiya is a contradiction to our proposition. Rather than be dismayed at the presence of a kushiya, we should welcome it as a gift because it will help guide us to the *emes*, the true explanation of the text.

How to Excel in Learning

This process is laid out clearly by the Ramchal in the first chapter of *Derech Tevunos*. This is what was done in the Yeshiva, both in the shiurim and outside the shiurim; in iyun and in b`kiyus. It is what best defines the derech halimud of the Yeshiva and what the Rosh HaYeshiva, *zt"l*, had in mind, in my opinion, when he said, "All the Yeshivos in Europe learned this way." It is my humble opinion that, without developing the ability to generate hypotheses and to test them, by definition, the learner cannot become a *lomdan*. At best he can attend shiurim without attaining a deep understanding. The Torah Hakedosha is deep and covered, and without a tool to penetrate the upper surface, how can one reach the true understanding?

After being exposed to this concept, one can recognize it being used throughout the Gemora and the commentaries. B`ezras Hashem, more will be spoken about this in the next section.

Both are the Words of the Living G-d

We have a tradition that Rashi had *Ruach HaKodesh*. If that is true, how is it possible for the Ba`alei HaTosfos, his own grandchildren, to disagree with him? Even if you will say that they also had Ruach HaKodesh, but he had lived in a previous generation! We can ask similarly on the Ramban on the Chumash, who consistently challenges and often dismisses Rashi`s position. We must conclude that the definition of Ruach HaKodesh cannot mean something like *Nevuah*, prophecy, by which the *Navi* reached the Ultimate of Truth and which would not be subject to challenge. Rather, the explanation stems from the fact that in order to arrive at a hypothesis to explain a topic of the Torah and to test it against all the other

How to Excel in Learning

relevant discussions in the Talmud, tremendous help from Heaven is required. Why? Because the talmid chachom has to remember all the discussions in the Talmud and then select those which are relevant. Furthermore, each of these discussions has many ways of viewing it. Realize that within each topic there are many disagreements in the Rishonim and Acharonim. After all this he must examine that his approach does not contradict any other sugya according to his stance on those sugyas. Finally, he must write in a way which will be understood. All this requires, D-vine Assistance on a level which is called Ruach HaKodesh. (When I said this over to my son, Moshe, may he have much success, he told me that the Ramban in *Milchamos Hashem*, writes that there is no sugya which has just one explanation.) Presumably, all the above applies to the words of a Tannah, Amorah, Rishon, or Acharon. If you think that their words are in the category of certainty, as in prophecy, then why do they have more than one answer to a question and why do they argue with each other? We must say that due to their broad knowledge of the Talmud, they develop many possible conclusions for one question or matter. If they present only one, it may be that they chose only one which they felt was the best of many possibilities. Therefore, Ruach HaKodesh is the assistance that someone receives in order that he doesn't stray from the path of logic. It is precisely because this path may lead to many conclusions that we see even one author will at times present many possible conclusions. However, to establish the Halacha, he must choose what he feels is the best possibility. Nevertheless, for learning, he is entitled to present all these viable possibilities since he doesn't know which of them is the Ultimate Truth.

Now we can begin to understand the statement of Chazal, "Both of their views are the Words of the Living G-d." Of course in a situation in which there is no contradiction between them there is no difficulty. But if there is a contradiction between them, how is it possible for both of them to be true? Did HaKodesh Baruch Hu give Moshe Rabbenu two Torahs?! Rather, as we just hinted before, since each has toiled to reach the truth and to test his hypothesis based on the entire Talmud, therefore both possibilities are worthy of being called "the Words of the Living G-d." In truth, this is what Hashem wants from us, to strive to come as close to the truth as possible according to our ability. From this point onwards, when I use the word *emes*, or truth, it is with this definition: it is, "the closest to the truth that one is able to come, given his abilities."

Despite all this, there are those who would like to describe the result of the previously mentioned process of textual analysis as truth. On this topic, it is helpful to refer to *Chidushei Haleiv* of the Rosh HaYeshiva, *zt"l,* on Parshas

How to Excel in Learning

Toledos (p.100) where he brings the Gemora, *Makkos* 23b:

Rebbi Elazar said: In three places the Ruach HaKodesh was revealed...[the third place was] in the court of Shlomo Hamelech, for it is written (*Malachim I* (3:27)) "And the king answered and he said, 'Give to her the living child and do not kill it. She is the mother.` How did he know? Maybe she was deceptively acting as a mother would? We must say that a Bas Kol said these words, "She is the mother."

The Rosh Ha Yeshiva, *zt"l*, explains, " We see that Rebbi Elazar asks, "How could he know decisively?" and he answers that Shlomo merely said, 'Give her the child, do not kill it' and the Bas Kol said the rest. The Rosh HaYeshiva, *zt"l*, continues, "It is surprising that the Shlomo HaMelech himself did not exclaim, 'She is the mother!' After all, he had pretty clear evidence for this conclusion. We must say therefore, that even if there is a remote chance that what we are about to say is not true, we must not say it as the emes. Although we may act according to this conclusion, as Shlomo did, nevertheless we cannot describe it as the unchallengeable truth."

Applying this to ourselves, who toil in Torah, after having striven and strained to reach the truth, devoting all of our abilities and resources towards this end, we may still not claim that in fact we have reached it. Rather, at most we can say, "This appears to me to be the correct explanation. Nevertheless, I am prepared to listen to any questions and comments that you may have and to modify it if necessary."

The Text and the Commentaries

There seems to be a widespread practice of talmidim who, when they are learning a text, immediately run to the commentaries. They feel

that they cannot understand what is written without the help of commentaries. This may be true in the final sense, but by not first attempting to figure out the p`shat by themselves, they are not using their own potential to the fullest extent. It also reduces the chances that they will understand the commentaries, who assume that the reader worked on the text beforehand. The first step should be to attempt to understand the text without assistance by reading it many times, each time identifying gaps in one`s comprehension and trying to fill them. With experience, one learns how many times and how much effort it takes to get a basic understanding and how much beyond the basic meaning one is capable of attaining.
Afterwards, it is time for the commentaries. Not all texts are equal on this point. It is often difficult to make clear progress in the text of the Gemora without Rashi. Nevertheless, glancing at Rashi should be held at a minimum. The key

to understanding the text fully depends upon how much patience the student has in re-reading both the text and the commentary, repeatedly going back and forth between them until all his uncertainties are clarified. It is very possible that it could take twenty or fifty readings just to gain a minimal p'shat. It should be understood that reading means that each word is read carefully as if it was the first and only time that it is being read, attempting to account for how each word and letter is necessary and how it fits into its precise place. If he is not successful, then he knows that an additional reading is called for. On this point, there is a difference between Rashi, (and whoever takes his place, such as the Rashbam on *Pesachim* and *Bava Basra*) and other commentaries. Generally, Rashi comes to the aid of a talmid who never learned the subject before, and to assist him in reading the text. This is not the case with other Rishonim, who come to prove their approach and to disprove alternative approaches. They are writing for another Rishon who knows the entire Talmud quite thoroughly. This is ample reason for learning Rashi before any other of the *m'forshim*. After comprehending Rashi's approach to the Gemora, then one can move to the other commentaries. The clearer one grasps the text, the clearer one will grasp the discussions on it. The sefer *Darchei HaGemora* goes into this in detail.

It follows from what we mentioned previously, that in order to attain the exact meaning of a *m'foresh* it is important to learn through the citations that he brings because he assumes that you understand them. To begin, one should skim through these references, but the clarity of a final p'shat depends upon the extent to which one has delved into these citations. Many times their quote does not encompass the entire relevant portion of the reference, but only the point which they are focusing on. In such cases it is imperative that one also sees the background material.

Preliminaries for Learning

The first step necessary for optimizing one's learning, *al pi teva*, is to be careful to get sufficient sleep at night. Lack of sufficient sleep adds unnecessary obstacles in the path of learning properly. The memory doesn't function as it should. Generally each day's shiur is built upon the previous day's shiur, so if one doesn't have complete immediate recall of the previous shiur, one is working with a handicap and may even lose the present shiur entirely. One lost shiur leads to another and then to another. We want to start a positive chain of events. The night before one should remind oneself that tomorrow's success in gaining clarity depends on tonight's sleep.

How to Excel in Learning

Adequate lighting is very important. It is best that the seforim have the largest fonts available. However, there are many seforim with very small print; good light removes unnecessary eye strain and preoccupation with the inconvenience of not being able to see clearly and easily.

Following are a number of points that I would like to mention which may appear to be very basic. However, I am including them because I have seen some who have come out against what I am recommending and others who have defended practices which I feel are not helpful and many who simple neglect these areas.

Straight posture is conducive to alertness. The sefer should be held at an angle of 90 degrees to the line of sight. A shtender helps fulfil these objectives. It is better that each student have his own chair rather than one bench for a number of students. In this way each student is not disturbed by the movements of the others. There should be adequate ventilation and it should not be too warm in order that it interferes with the students' alertness.

The text itself should be as large a print that you can obtain in order to avoid unnecessary eyestrain which can distract one's concentration. Always look inside the text unless you already memorized it. Otherwise, your mind may be occupied trying just to remember the details instead of straining to understand them.

Learning with a *Chavrusa*

The goal of learning with a chavrusa is not to teach him. That is the responsibility of his

Rebbi. Each should ask the other what he does not know and answer his questions. The Rosh HaYeshiva, *zt"l*, would relate how once he was learning with a chavrusa and the chavrusa asked him a *kushiya*. He answered him based on a p`shat of a *daf* that they had learned previously.  The chavrusa then asked him why he had not told him that p`shat at the time when they had learned it. The Rosh HaYeshiva, *zt"l*, answered him that it was because the chavrusa had not asked The Rosh HaYeshiva, *zt"l* when they had first learned it. The point being that although the goal of the student is to know whatever he is learning as clearly as possible, it is not a proper goal to make sure everyone else also does. That is the responsibility of the Rosh HaYeshiva and Rebbeim. If a talmid attempts to worry about his chavrusa, he may end up insulting his chavrusa, in addition to slowing down their progress. Of course, if the chavrusa requests that he drill him and to make sure to tell him all his ideas then he certainly can try it.

Choosing a Chavrusa

The major issue when choosing a chavrusa is whether he should be stronger or weaker in learning than you. The advantage of his being stronger is that you can learn a lot of information and techniques. The advantage if he is weaker is that you must work harder. If you need information you can ask the more advanced talmidim. In any event, one can switch off on subsequent *z'manim*.

The second major issue is their style. Some like to speak out what they are thinking. Others prefer to think before they speak. If both chavrusos have the same style, it will be easier to function together. If they have opposite styles it may be frustrating for both.

The third matter is communication skill. If, for whatever reason, there is a communication problem, whether it is due to lack of audibility, choice of vocabulary, or language, it must be taken into account.

Preparation for the Shiur

By all accounts, proper preparation is a key element in gaining success.

To a large extent, the success of learning depends on one's attitude in preparation. Just looking at the text to be familiar with it will not be as effective as trying to determine the p`shat, the meaning of the text before coming to shiur. Try to come prepared knowing completely what your Rebbi will say, regardless of how many times in the past you didn't achieve this. Every day one should say, "Today with Hashem's help I will reach clarity of my

How to Excel in Learning

Rebbi before I come to shiur." It is very helpful to record your ideas before going to shiur (as will B`ezras Hashem be discussed in the section on Note Taking). If this is done, one will avoid thinking that he already knew the p`shat of the Rebbi when in fact he did not. This will enable him to search and determine where he went astray and then to be prepared against making that error in the future. If he doesn`t write it down, there is a tendency to feel that what the Rebbi is saying is also what he thought before. This in part is due to his mind still being untrained to recognize the slight nuances of different concepts.

Before beginning learning, one should always clarify what his immediate goal is. Is it to learn in depth, to cover ground, or to memorize? Which text is he learning in this session? How much of the text is he supposed to prepare?

How to Excel in Learning

These questions will help focus his efforts so that he can be best prepared for the shiur.

Never come late to shiur! You will be starting with an unnecessary handicap if you must use your talents to try to figure out what the Rebbi had said before you came, especially if it is at the same time that you are trying to listen to what he is saying now. This is true even if he did not actually say anything but you merely think he did! Therefore, make sure not to compromise on being present so you can hear the first words he says.

Taking Notes

When I have asked individuals how many sets of notes a talmid should have for each shiur, the usual response I have received indicates that the individual never thought seriously about

How to Excel in Learning

this question before. What answer would you give? Before presenting my answer, let us first mention a few general points about taking notes. First of all, in general, all notes should be in ink since pencil often fades and becomes illegible. The pen itself should allow you to write quickly and smoothly and the thickness of the point should enable you to read the writing comfortably. As to which type of notebook is best, loose-leaf papers can tear out and their order can only be determined easily if they are numbered on a consistent basis. A cloth-bound notebook is often awkward when space is limited and it also has the tendency of closing by itself. For these reasons a spiral bound notebook is recommended as most suitable. One should not type notes unless one is an accomplished typist because otherwise it will slow down this entire process.

If you decide to write directly into your Gemorah it should be limited to three types of information. The first is translation of words.

This should be at the bottom of the page for two reasons. First, this will avoid cluttering up the text. Secondly, it will give you a chance to use your memory before you inadvertently look at the translations. Having the translation of unfamiliar words saves you the time of having to look them up. The second type of annotation is reference to other sources. These should be placed alongside the point in the text to which they comment on. An asterisk, a dot system, or footnote type numbers will help identify to which point in the text each reference corresponds to. The third possibility is when one wants to write concise comments while one is learning *bekius*. All these notes should be in ink for the same reason mentioned previously.

Detailed Note-Taking Plan

The importance of writing notes as concisely as possibly cannot be over-emphasized. In fact, the success of note-taking largely depends on how concise one's notes are. They should be in a your own shorthand in order to minimize the interference with the natural flow of discussions between the chavrusas, or between the talmid and Rebbi, or to listening to the Rebbi's shiur. The general format should be in an outline form. For quickly locating the major points, a system of identifying abbreviations should be used. For example, questions can be highlighted with a "Q," answers with an "A," kushiyas with a "K," Rabbi with an "R," and with as "w/." The first question can be identified as "Q1." The advantage of numbering the questions and answers is that it allows for rapid organization of the ideas. Just think of the following scenario: as you are quickly jotting down four answers to question two, suddenly two answers to question number one occur to you and there is only enough space for one answer before your series of answers to question two begin. This situation is easily solvable by using proper identification of each point, since even if it is not in the correct sequence or order on the page, you will know where each point belongs.

For example, by writing A_Q21 and A_Q22, you can immediately know that these are two answers to Question 2 and not one answer to the first question and the other to the second. Identification in this manner frees the talmid from the constraints of a strict outline numbering system that can lead to misinterpretation or slowed comprehension. Use numbers and letters for making insertions of ideas or for re-establishing the order and flow of the ideas or sections. All these techniques contribute to maximizing the speed in which the student can assemble and test a maximum number of hypotheses in a short time period. In the final form you will be able to write every point in its proper place. One should not worry that the notes will be unintelligible in less than a week. The assumption is that you will decipher them before that time and then rewrite them.

How to Excel in Learning

Now let us first develop the system. In order to reap the most from a shiur, regardless of the give and take that occurs during the lesson, one must prepare beforehand. During that preparation it is ideal to attempt to understand the text using one's own capabilities. Since there are many variations and alternatives on how to understand each of the many points contained in the texts assigned for a particular day, the variations of combinations quickly escalate. Instead of feeling confused and overwhelmed, taking notes can help focus and give order to these numerous ideas that have yet to be developed. Specifically, these are the hypotheses that must be tested, as mentioned in the section on Recognizing the Logic Used in Learning. After recording his own ideas separately or along with those of his study partner, the chavrusas can begin to exam the merits of each item in turn. Thus the *first* set of notes includes his initial ideas. After examining

Rashi and/or Tosfos, he should incorporate his understanding of these commentaries into his first set of notes, adding them in wherever necessary. Of course, this may include a number of variations on each Rishon's comment. If the reader is wondering about the necessity of such laborious work, one of the benefits is the *chizuk* and satisfaction he'll experience upon seeing at least one, if not many, of his varying ideas discussed among the Acharonim mentioned in shiur or in the seforim. The major benefit, however, is that this method forces him to clarify the topic at hand. This is the goal of iyun: that he reaches the ultimate clarity that he is capable of achieving.

The *second* set of notes contains the conclusions drawn by the end of his discussion with his chavrusa, namely, those original ideas which were not discarded as flawed. As mentioned before, these notes must be concise. With these ideas he is ready to enter the shiur.

The shiur itself requires its own record. It is advisable to keep a separate notebook. Merely using a separate section in the same notebook in which the preparation notes are located makes it difficult to compare the two sets of notes, since the two sections cannot both be open at the same time. Being able to compare the two will save the need to start from scratch again. Obviously, notes taken during shiur must be jotted down very rapidly. Therefore lines should be skipped so that immediately after the class the student can add in as much as necessary so that at the next review session he will be able to further reconstruct the contents of the shiur. This review should be as soon as possible. Taking five minutes right after shiur may save considerable time, rather than if he first reviews them an hour or two later. By the next day, it may be too late to accurately rebuild the discussion from these terse recordings; therefore every effort must be made to rewrite them on the same day, as soon as possible. This is the *third* set of notes.

Now the *fourth* set, the *chazara* . This is the time to work out step by step what the Rebbi said. Even if you do not understand the connections between the steps, write each step down, leaving blank spaces wherever you feel you are missing some point. After you have all the steps, analyze the connections. If you do not understand the connections, ask your Rebbi. Now you can easily insert those crucial steps, which were previously missed, into those blank lines. After you understand the entire discussion, you can go back to your original ideas and analyze why the Rebbi didn't say it the way you thought it should be. If you cannot figure it out, ask.

How to Excel in Learning

After you understand the entire flow of the discussion you are ready to write the final form in a clear handwriting or to type it. This is the copy that can be referred to during all future reviews. Needless to say, space should be left to allow for inserting additional insights on those subsequent sessions. If the final copy is on a computer disk, then these last step is done automatically. By now we have a *fifth* copy of the shiur.

This procedure is well worth the time because it develops one's ability to think through a thought chain necessary for understanding any sugya in Shas. It forces one to learn how to focus one's thoughts and increases one's attention span as well as depth.

The beginner must be aware that he is not expected to complete the above regime on the first day. If previously he never succeeded in recording anything during shiur, then on the first day if he is now able to record one line in the middle of the lesson, that is progress. Gradually, day-by-day, week-by-week he will be able to write down greater percentages of the lesson, until, with Hashem's help, he will succeed in being able to write a complete copy of the shiur.

Summarizing: we have five basic sets of notes: 1) initial ideas before the shiur, 2) conclusions before shiur, 3) notes written during the shiur, 4) review session, and 5) the final version.

Participation During the Shiur

The talmid must strive to hear every word that the Rebbi says. It is best to try to have all of his questions answered immediately while the question is still fresh in his mind. If he doesn`t understand the answer, he should tell the Rebbi so, until he understands. He should not be concerned that he is taking time away from his peers, because they may not have the answers either. Furthermore, the Rebbi will decide if the question is not consistent with the goals of the shiur. Only if the Rebbi says that they must move on should he stop and save the discussion for after the shiur. It is worthwhile to quickly jot down the answer even if it delays the discussion of the shiur a few seconds more.

Wherever there is an opportunity to ask questions the student should be aware of the fact that the more developed the question is, the more it can lead to a useful answer. The more the question remains vague, the more it leads to a vague answer. Part of the toil in learning is putting in the effort to clarify the question. Often this enables the talmid to answer his own question.

Criticism

Chiddushim that occur to the talmid are good starting points to pursue and investigate their validity. However, there are young students who feel that any idea that formulates in their minds must be *emes* and a product of *Ruach HaKodesh* and that, *chas v`sholom* anyone should dare challenge them. Perhaps this feeling stems from *gaivah,* self-pride. It is true that these thoughts are matanos *min HaShamayim*. Furthermore, it is to the great credit and merit of that student that he has these ideas. However, they are only stepping stones upon which to build. They must be worked on in order to ascertain which parts should be kept, which parts should be modified, and which parts should be set aside in the meantime. This is exactly the work that must be done in preparing any *chaburah* or chiddush.

Concerning criticism from the Rebbim towards the talmidim, I do not recall hearing that the Rosh HaYeshiva, *zt"l*, would sit and listen to *avreichim* delivering chaburas. When someone of advanced level sits in on a chabura, it tends to add tension to the one presenting the chaburah. If this will interfere with his ability to concentrate it is not a productive arrangement.

The solution I advocate is that, within the framework of the Yeshiva and not the Kollel, the shiur be the place where constructive criticism takes place. Then, even if he is presenting something that a talmid suggested, the Rebbi is under attack and not the talmid, which spares the talmid embarrassment, or at least mitigates it. But certainly, when the Rebbi is presenting an idea and the talmid questions or attacks it, his defense is really a constructive critic on the talmid, but in a way in which the talmid feels it much less. Of course in order to achieve this, the Rebbi must not insult them even in a subtle way and certainly not outright. He must take their suggestions with respect and seriousness. In addition, what an avreich says for his chabura is generally the fruit of much more labor and emotion than what a bochur says in shiur, so therefore the bochur is less likely to be hurt as much as an avreich. If the avereich continues and eventually gives a shiur, he will then receive feedback from his talmidim. If, however, an avreich insists on the analysis of the Rosh HaYeshiva or Rosh Kollel, then by all means this talmid should be developed.

How to Excel in Learning

Disagreeing with the Rebbi

We see in *Bava Basra* 130b that Rav Huna the son of Rava said to his talmidim that if they did not understand his psak then in an identical situation, but with different people, they had his permission to pasken as they wished. Only with regard to those same people would it be forbidden to pasken differently and thereby void the p`sak of their Rebbi, because of the requirement of properly honoring their Rebbi. All the more so with learning. A talmid must ask his questions on his Rebbi in order that he understand what he saying. The Rosh HaYeshiva, Rabbi Moshe Dov Chait,zt"l, would quote Reb Dovid*, zt"l*, as having said that if the talmidim are listening to the Rebbi and they are agreeing with him, it is a sign that they really do not understand him. In *Or Yisroel*, letter 6, the author writes, "This is how *Chazal* taught us to behave, as related in *Kiddushin* 30 `Even a father and son, a Rebbi and his talmid, learning in one gate, become enemies,` this initial strife refers to learning with sharpness." In the *Perush*, HaRav Uri Weisblum, *shlita*, explains that they are guiding us in the proper way to learn and that despite the son being commanded to honor his father and the student his teacher, they are obligated to have animosity between them, because otherwise, it is not called learning. Afterwards he brings the source that it is forbidden to disagree with an expert Judge (*Sanhedrin* 36). He explains that this reference is speaking about a *p`sak din* and not about learning. It is understandable that all the criticism mentioned above must be with respect and friendliness. That is the way it was in the Yeshiva when I learned there.

Review of the Shiur

It seems that some students feel that *lomdas* comes from free thinking. They do not

How to Excel in Learning

appreciate that the path of the commentaries of the previous generations has been to invest much effort in making sure all the logical steps of the discussion were precisely grasped before introducing any novel ideas. Harav HaGaon Rabbi Shmuel Niman, *zt"l*, would often remind his talmidim that lomdas is 90% *cheshbon*, that is making sure that all the steps were logical and that they were in their logical order. Only the last 10% is the development of a novel explanation. In order to build the ability to think logically it imperative for the student to review with comprehension what someone with an advanced level of logic says. This should be the major goal of review. The practical application of this is to strive to be able to repeat over the shiur without the assistance of notes. In the initial stage, being able to cover a few points is enough to merit being called a "success." Just doing this may take more time than he can allocate (for example, because he must learn *b`kiyus* with a chavrusa) that he cannot encompass the entire contents of the shiur. If he can free himself from other obligations, then it is worthwhile to spend his entire day reconstructing what transpired in the shiur. Of course, this assumes that he will be able to use out the entire day working on this with enthusiasm. If it leads to day dreaming, or other *b'tala*, he is not ready for this, and should not drop his other agenda.

It is only a secondary purpose to imbibe knowledge of the material that was discussed in shiur.

Use of Recorders

The first fundamental point in using a recorder is to listen to shiur as if you did not have a recorder. Otherwise you are training yourself not to listen and if that is the case, it is probably better not to use it at all. The purpose of using a recorder is to help you with what you missed during shiur even though you were trying to catch everything. The recorder becomes very powerful for someone who despite all his attention and concentration during the shiur, leaves with very little. Instead of trying to find someone to repeat the entire lesson over, the recording allows him to hear it again, this time at his own suitable speed.

The second fundamental point is active listening. The goal here is to transcribe the entire shiur. This approach requires the listener to define the true meaning intended by the speaker for each word and sentence. Even if it appears to consume a lot of time to establish this, the investment is worth it. Words which he missed during the shiur may have been due to their being beyond his vocabulary or not according to his familiar usage. Now he can look them up or take the time to think through multiple possibilities to ascertain the intention of the speaker. The more he uses out his potential, the more he will sharpen his abilities. This process will help develop the ability to understand what is being said even as it is being said. It is very likely that he will eventually be fast enough to ask the Rebbi his questions during the shiur.

Just as note taking, the ability to transcribe is one which is gradually developed. If you don't have the time to go through the entire shiur, just do as much as you can. If you have the precious opportunity to spend the entire day on transcribing it, that would be very valuable. Remember that each stage is success, starting from writing one line and gradually progressing to a number of lines. Afterwards one is able to say over with looking at notes and then eventually without looking.

How to Excel in Learning

Remembering by Heart

Although this topic is not the central theme of this guide, for completeness I would like to touch upon it. The more one makes this topic his major concern, the more it has the potential to distract him from all the other goals mentioned in this guide, so it should be approached with caution.

It is recommended that the talmid read Rabbi Yehoshua Cohen's *Kerem Yehoshua*. Also Rabbi Sender Dolgin, *shlita,* founder of Chaburas Shas, can be contacted about his approach to remembering Shas, which he feels is accessible to everyone. Each have different approaches to being able to remember what one learns.

How to Excel in Learning

Use of Time

In order to use your time effectively it can be helpful to divide your time into smaller intervals. For example, if you have an hour, you could allocate ten minutes for skimming the text, then fifteen minutes for determining a tentative hypothesis of the structure, a half hour to thinking about each detail, and the last five minutes to review your conclusions. When confronted with an entire z'man, you should divide it into smaller segments. For example, the winter z'man should be divided after the month of Elul, with special effort between Rosh Hashona and Yom Kippur, from Cheshvan to Chanuka, making a special effort before Chanuka. Then from Chanuka to Purim and Purim to Pesach. Remember each Yom Tov contains themes related directly to learning Torah and therefore one should try to inaugurate the day after having striven to attain greater achievements during the weeks before.

For example, the time between Pesach and Shevuos leads up to Kabbalos HaTorah, so it is a time to reach for new levels of understanding. During "Bein hamitzryim" is a time to correct, "Because they forsook My Torah." The idea is to always divide up the larger quantities of time into smaller sections and to focus on those smaller slots.

Using Tutors to Your Best Advantage

If the talmid can keep up with the class, then the tutor is for enrichment. However, if the talmid is over-whelmed by the class requirements, tutors should go at the speed of the talmid, they should generally not be used to keep the weak student up with the rest of class. He could not keep up during the class, so why should he be dragged through the same ordeal a second time?! After going at the student's speed for weeks or months he will be built up. At that point it can be experimented as to whether he is able to go at the speed of his peers. One should strive to have the tutoring at the time of the regular classes in order to avoid overburdening the talmid by reducing his free time further. The tutor should give the talmid the chance to work out the problems and the solutions rather than spoon feed him.

Listening to Lectures

A lecture is a presentation in which the talmidim cannot interact with the speaker. Therefore, many of the points mentioned in connection to a shiur cannot apply. One essential proactive technique is to strive to determine the structure of the presentation as the lecturer is speaking. If the lecture is on

Shabbos try to keep repeating this structure to yourself, building as the speaker continues to speak.

Originating Chidushim

This topic is not really a new one, but rather an extension of what has been already discussed throughout this guide. If something is difficult or troubling to the talmid, chances are that it can be developed into a chiddish. The Steiple Rav, zt"l, defined a chiddish as something new to the talmid. Some seem to feel that they must invent something so new that it was never said before. If that were true then they would be searching for something that Hashem did not even tell to Moshe! Rather, the goal should be to first identify a point which is unclear or which seems to be self-contradictory or other information, and then work to answer the problem. Thus one should focus on a limited area and strive to define and strengthen the difficulty. It is best to concentrate on clarifying the comments of a Rishon, Acharon, or Rosh HaYeshiva, rather than the Gemora itself. The chiddish doesn't necessarily have to contain an answer, sometimes merely leaving a well-defined kushiya, if it is a good one, may also be enough.

Delivering a Chabura

The goal of presenting a chabura, is to say your chiddish in front of your peers. They will generally think of points and weaknesses that you didn't. One pitfall is feeling that you must convince the audience that your chiddish is correct. First of all, it may not be. Second of all, even if it is, there is a natural skepticism and reluctance of the listeners to admit that something that they did not think of is emes.

How to Excel in Learning

You can reduce this negativism by asking many lead up questions. However, you may not succeed. Therefore, one's goal should to present your questions and answers clearly and try checking to see if they understand them. One should also try to answer any questions that they have on your questions or answers. But you should avoid cycling through an endless series of rebuttals and counter rebuttals or a standoff. That could be done later, but not during the limited time allotted for a chabura. This advice I received from HaRav HaGaon Rabbi Avrahom Kanerek, *shlita*, If those who were challenging you are not willing to discuss it with you privately, it proves that during the chabura they were really not open to hearing what you had to say and you would never have been able to succeed in convincing them then, and probably not in the future either.

These last two sections pave the way for the next section.

How to Teach According to this Derech

Until now the discussion was essentially directed towards the talmid. This section is for the Rebbi. First of all, it says in *Pirkei Avos* (4:15) "Rabbi Elazar ben Shamua says,`Let the honor of your talmid be just as dear to you as your own `." It is upon the Rebbi to be very, very careful of not embarrassing a bochur or an avreich of any age or any level. There is ample embarrassment if the Rebbi asks a kushiya on the student`s words, so what is the purpose of adding to this?

There are two fundamental ways for a Rebbi to make his students happy for a limited time. Either he gives a lecture in which they are not permitted to interrupt; this way they have nothing to be afraid of since there is no chance that they will make a mistake and be embarrassed. The second way is that there is

How to Excel in Learning

no responsibility on the student to comprehend what the Rebbi is saying, and it is sufficient for them to say to the Rebbi something that is similar to what he said. This approach has no opening for criticism, just encouragement. Then there is another way, a third possibility, which is a combination of the first two. Here there is the opportunity for both the Rebbi as well as the talmidim to speak during the shiur. However, they are really not speaking to each other because neither is really trying to understand the other. The problem with the first way is that there is no motivation for the students to listen so they generally won't do it so well. Since they don't speak, the Rebbi has no way of figuring out where they are weak so he can't help them. The shortcoming of the second way is that they do not hear comments from the Rebbi, so even if he is aware of their mistakes, he doesn't actually assist them.

Nevertheless, where both the Rebbim and the talmidim have lofty aspirations and burning desires to become astute in delving into the depths on a high plateau, and understandably this also requires a great amount of patience or at least developing it, then the best option is that the talmid listen in a way that in the final stage he can write up the shiur and say it, at least with his notes. Then afterwards he says it over to the Rebbi, where the Rebbi agrees when he is right, and where he is not, the Rebbi guides him to find the correct answers by questioning him.

If we agree that there is a responsibility on the Rebbi to help the talmid to develop in all the avenues that we have mentioned previously, then we must say that his job is not merely to present what the talmid could read by himself, but rather to guide and train him to become accustomed to search behind what is written. This is what Reb Dovid, *zt"l* used to say, "We must read between the lines." It seems that the explanation is to fill the space between the lines with kushiyos and teruztim according to the

How to Excel in Learning

rules of the sefer *Darkei HaGemora*. His policy should be not to tell the talmid before trying to pull out a kushiya, a terutz, or a s`vora from the mouth and mind of the talmid first. The main job of the Rebbi is to present the topic so clearly to the talmid, that the talmid will see the pressing kushiya and, later, the correct answer.

How can the Rebbi get to this level? If he knows the sugya thoroughly, then he will be able to guide the talmidim by questioning them with the type of questions outlined in *Darchei HaGemora*. The goal is that via the questions of the Rebbi, the talmid will use his own abilities to attain the *kushiyos* and the *teruztim*. Then he will truly understand what is being said. It goes without saying that even if the student says the right thing, the Rebbi must investigate whether he actually understands the words that he is mouthing. It not necessary (and not possible) to question every student during the course of one shiur, but there should be time allocated each day to at least spot check, if not all, at least a percentage of the tamidim. If he can`t, it is a sign that his shiur is too big and/or he is going too fast. If he cannot do this, then he needs assistants who are experts in his shiur to do it. Then the next day he must ascertain if the talmidim are with him by briefly reviewing the previous shiur or by seeing if they follow the next day`s shiur.

Whenever he sees that they are stuck, he should not give them the answer, whether that answer is a question, answer, or concept, but rather he must provide an introductory step to help them get to point that he wants them to see. With time they will eventually use their time to reach these points without his help. Then he will know that he was successful. At that time, he can raise the level of the shiur. When they are thinking on their own he can begin to throw out questions during the shiur leaving them for the talmidim to work on during preparation.

How to Excel in Learning

Understandably, if the Rebbi presents the results of his toils, without explaining how he arrived there, the usefulness of his shiur is rather minimal because how are they going to figure out how he got there. If they can, maybe they don't really need his shiur. On the other hand, if he enters into all the details of the language, but without exposing all the difficulties in the text, the talmidim may not appreciate how much effort it took to reach the final p'shat. This is not the case when he brings them along the entire rough path. Then they can understand that in order to reach the final destination much toil is necessary. They also have a personal example of how to analyze the text.

Generally, Pilpul Shiurim and Shiur Klali are not open for comments by the talmidim because the Rosh HaYeshiva or Magid Shiur has an agenda which he wants to accomplish during the allotted time. One of the goals is to demonstrate to the talmidim the extent of the depth that can be reached, which is especially important in a Yeshiva that has a thorough derech in which not too many siyums are made. Even so, there still is a way in which it can be done whereby the talmidim will not feel overwelmed. The Rosh HaYeshiva, *zt"l*, would choose topics which were related to what the Yeshiva had already invested a few weeks of learning in. He would provide the b`nei HaYeshiva with all the material that was to be presented and they had at least three days to prepare. After the shiur, they had an additional three days to review it. The Rosh HaYeshiva, *zt"l*, would host sessions in which the talmidim could discuss the points which still needed clarification. In this way, the talmidim came to the shiurim charged with enthusiasm and they grew dramatically from the experience.

Asking a Posek

After one examines this guide, it is possible that the reader will be unsure as to whether or not he should change from the particular path of learning that he finds himself in. He may be inclined to ask one of the *Gadolei HaDor* what he should do. For this he must know how to ask a *sheila*. Certainly if he asks whether he should learn all of Shas, or all day, or all his life, he will receive a bracha. However, to receive advice he must explain what his abilities are and what his true aspirations are. He must reveal the extent to which he is prepared to sacrifice in order to reach that goal. He could ask what is proper for him now, to perfect his understanding and to work on iyun and at the same time to present an example of his level. He could ask, for example, that since his memory is weak, is it worth devoting his energies and most of his time learning Shas. In short, he needs to go into details in order to receive an appropriate p`sak and not just a bracha, which of course is valuable, but it is not guidance.

The reason for this is that one who comes to ask, but really is seeking honor, is not prepared to accept advice which would go against his desires. Therefore, the Gadol feels there is no purpose to tell him directly and that it is better that he learn from life, because if he was told directly, chances are that he would not listen to the advice of the Gadol. Refusing to listen would not be to his credit. Also, a Gadol cannot impose on a talmid to embark on a difficult path even if this is the best thing for him. The talmid must show that he is ready for it by showing the degree that he wants it.

Let us close with a Bracha:

May Hashem bestow Bracha and Hatzlacha on all who seek to learn His Torah.

Glossary

Acharon: later commentary; (plural: Acharonim)

amkan: deep thinker

b`ezras : with the help

b`kiyus: broad knowledge

b`nei HaYeshiva: refers to the Rebbim, talmidim, and alumni of the Yeshiva

b`tala: waste of time

baki: one with broad knowledge of the Torah;(plural: b`kiyim)

ba`al middos tovos: someone with exemplary character traits

bochur: young man; (plural: bochurim)

chabura: a lecture prepared and presented by a student to his peers

chazara: review of study material

How to Excel in Learning

Chazal: Chachameinu Zichronom Livracha, our Sages of blessed memory

chinuch habonim: education of children

chizuk: strength, encouragement

daf: page, usually referring to the Talmud;(plural: dapim)

darshan: lecturer on ethics

daven: pray

derech halimud: approach to learning

emes: truth

emunah: belief in Hashem

Gadol: giant, used here to refer to one of the Torah leaders towards whom all the Roshei HaYeshiva, Rabbis, Rebbeim, and Observant lay community look for guidance ; (plural: Gadolim)

gaivah: self-pride

Gemora: discussion part of the Talmud

How to Excel in Learning

Halacha: ruling on Torah law

HaMelech: the King

Hashem: G-d

kushiya: a contradiction

kollel: institute for men learning Torah

lemud: learning

lomdan: one who knows how to learn Torah in depth

magid shiur: the who says the shiur, the teacher

Maran: our teacher

matana: gift

m`foresh: commentary; (plural: m`forshim)

middah: character trait; (plural: middos)

mussar: study of ethics

p`shat: the simple meaning of the text

How to Excel in Learning

p`sak: decision on the Halacha

pasken: to render a p`sak

pasuk: verse

perek: chapter

Poseik: one who decides Halacha issues, also one who is familiar with the decisions of Poskim (plural), even if doesn`t decide issues himself.

Rebbe: teacher of Torah subjects (plural: Rebbeim)

Rosh HaYeshiva: Dean, head of Yeshiva; (plural: Roshei HaYeshiva)

Rishon: earlier commentary; (plural Rishonim):

ruchniyos: spiritual

s`vara: a line of reasoning

sheila: question, often referring to what one asks a Gadol HaDor or a Posek

Siyata D`shmaya: help from Heaven

sefer: book

seminary: girls` school

shiur: class material ; (plural: shiurim)

shmuz: lecture, usually used together with Mussar, i.e. Mussar shmuz; (plural: shmuzim or shmuzen)

sugya: topic in the Talmud

talmid : student; (plural: talmidim)

teretz: answer; (plural: teruztim).

Torah Sh`ba`al Peh: Oral Law

yeshiva: school for learning Torah

yiras Sh`mayim: fear or awe of Heaven

z'man: time period, semester

How to Excel in Learning

Table of Contents of Emrei Chayil

<u>פתיחה</u>

א. הודיה להקב"ה, להורי ולרבותי
ב. השגחות פרטיות
ג. עידוד לתלמידים
ד. השקפה בענין תורה ומקצוע
ה. דרך הלימוד בישיבת חפץ חיים
ו. אודות עריכת הספר
ז. הדרך ללמידת הספר

<u>דרכי לימוד מרבותינו</u>

א. ספר דרכי הגמרא לרבינו יצחק ב"ר קנפנטון
ב. קצת דרכי עיון מהגאון מרן בעל "חזון איש"
ג. תמצית מתוך הספר דרכי הגמרא

<u>הדרך להצליח בלימוד</u>

א. פתח דברים
ב. מידות
ג. מטרת הלימוד בישיבה
ד. דרך הלימוד בישיבת חפץ חיים
ה. בקיאות ועמקות
ו. חשיבותה לנתוח כל מילה
ז. רמות בהבנת הלימוד
ח. זיהוי הלוגיקה שבה השתמשו בלימוד
ט. אלו ואלו דברי אלקים חיים
י. הכתוב והמפרשים
יא. ההכנות ללימוד
יב. לימוד עם חברותא

How to Excel in Learning

יג. בחירות חברותא
יד. הכנה לשיעור
יה. סיכומים
יו. תלמיד בזמן שיעור
יז. ביקורת
יח. תלמיד חולק על רבו
יט. חזרה
כ. הקלטה
כא. שינון בע"פ
כב. ניצול מירבי של הזמן
כג. לימוד עם מורה פרטי לתועלתך המירבית
כד. האזנה לדרשות
כה. לחדיש חידוש
כו. למסור החבורה
כז. כיצד ללמד לפי דרך הזה
כח. שאלת רב
מראה מקומות נוספים

ביבליוגרפיה יעילה

1. מוטיבציה
2. תרגום המינוחים
3. טכניקות

<u>מתמטיקה יסודית</u>

אלגברה
יסודית

גאומטרי
ה יסודית
טריגונומטריה
יסודית

How to Excel in Learning

ברכות

א. (דף לד:) הלכות תפילה
ב. הערות על דף מח.

שבת

ג. (שבת ב.) פירושו של "בפנים" ושל "בחוץ"
ד. בענין לומדים אבות מלאכות שבת מהמשכן
ה. (שבת ג.) העושה את כל המלאכה ולא רק מקצתה, ויחיד חייב, שנים פטורים מקצת מלאכה ולפתור סתירה בין הסוגיות
ו. פרושים של רש"י ותוס' על "פטורי דאתי לידי חיוב חטאת"
ז. עקירת גופו
ח. (שבת ג:) סוגיא של מי קנסוה רבנן לאהדורי לגביה
ט. (שבת ד.) רדיית הפת
י. (שבת ד.) קלוטה
יא. זורק ומושיט
יב. בענין אורחיה
יג. בענין הגדילו המידות
יד. (שבת יח:) חתוי גחלים והגסה
טו. (שבת כט,לא) מלאכה שאינו צריכה לגופה
טז. (שבת לו:) המבשל בשבת
יז. (שבת לז.) לסמוך
יח. בענין איסור רחיצה בשבת וביום טוב
יט. בענין מכבין גחלת של מתכת
כ. בענין חזרה
כא. מחלוקת בין מג"א ובין הגר"א ובאור הלכה
כב. הקשה לפי' רש"י על ההיתר של הכל בו
כג. רותחת להתיר חזרה
כד. פירוש של העולת שבת ברבינו ירוחם
כה. פירוש הרמ"א ברבינו ירוחם
כו. תרוץ שאין סתירה ברמ"א
כז. (שבת מט.,נא.) בסיס לדבר האסור
כח. (שבת צב:) מסייע

How to Excel in Learning

כט. (שבת מב.) מכבין גחלת של מתכת
ל. (שבת קו:) צידה
לא. פרק רביעי במה טומנין
לב. בענין בורר
לג. (כריתות פרק ד' משנה ג') מתעסק בכל התורה

עירובין

לד. (דף יג:) העורה על קורה עגולה
לה. (דף מה.) מחלוקת בין מג״א ובין הגר״א ובאור הלכה
לו. הערה על דף נו:
לז. (עירובין עו.) חלון עגול
לח. (עירובין צה.) המציל תפילין בשבת

פסחים

לט. (דף ב) פרושו של "אור"
מ. (דף ה:) פני יהושע ד״ה פרש״י ש״מ
מא. (דף ו:) טעם של בטול בלילה
מב. חתם סופר דף ו: ד״ה וכי משכחת לי׳ לבטלי׳
מג. (פסחים ח.) בענין בדיקת חמץ
מד. המהרש״א בדף ט' על המשנה
מה. (דף יב.) זמן ביעור
מו. חתם סופר או״ח סימן קנא
מז. רב חיים הלוי, זצ״ל, סימן א' בחמץ ומצוה
מח. (דף נח) המנחת חינוך מצוה ט׳, מצות השבתת חמץ, אות א'
מט. (דף קח:) בענין ארבע כוסות
נ. (דף קח:) פטרתן מלומר מה נשתנה
נא. (דף קט.) תוס' ד״ה רביעית של תורה אצבעים
נב. (פסחים קיד.) מצות צריכות כוונה
נג. (דף קיד:) באר תוס' ד״ה זאת אומרת
נד. (דף קטז.) שאלות מה נשתנה
נה. הערות על הדפים

How to Excel in Learning

ראש השנה

נו. (דף כח.) הנאה במקום מתעסק

יומא

נז. (דף כב.) התינוקות

סוכה

נח. (סוכה ז:) סוכה ככבשן
נט. (ט.) מי שגזל סכך
ס. (סוכה יז:) לבוד

ביצה

סא. (דף ב:) מוקצה
סב. (ביצה ג.) אוכלא דאפרת
סג. (דף ג.) נולד
סד. (דף יד:) בורר ביום טוב
סה. (דף יד) טלטול מוקצה
סו. (דף כו.) ההבדל בן נולד ובן ניכור
סז. (דף כו:) מוקצה לחצי שבת

כתובות

סח. (דף ב.) סיבת תקנת יום הרביעי
סט. (דף ב:) טענת אונס בגיטין (ברכת שמואל)

How to Excel in Learning

יבמות

ע. הערה על דף ג.
עא. (דף ג:) עשה דוחה לא תעשה שבכרת
עב. בעלת תנאי
עג. צרת ערוה
עד. פטור ערוה מיבום
עה. (דף ח.) סוגיא דתרי איסורי
עו. בירורים על ברכת שמואל סימן ה' - בענין צרת איילונית
עז. (דף יז:)דרכי נועם
עח. (דף לב.) איסור מוסיף ואיסור כולל
עט. (דף לה:) יבמתו ונמצאת מעוברת
פ. (דף י.) הסברה בתוס' ד"ה לעולם
פא. הערה על דף מא:
פב. הערה על דף נא.
פג. הערה על דף סו.
פד. הערה על דף סז.
פה. הערה על דף עא.
פו. הערה על דף פב.
פז. הערה על דף פח:
פח. הערה על דף צב:
פט. הערה על דף צד:
צ. הערה על דף צה:
צא. הערה על דף צח:
צב. הערה על דף צט.
צג. הערה על דף קד:
צד. הערה על דף קה.
צה. הערה על דף קז.
צו. הערה על דף קז:
צז. הערה על דף קט.
צח. הערה על דף קט:
צט. הערה על דף קי:
ק. הערה על דף קיא:
קא. הערה על דף קיג.
קב. הערה על דף קטו.
קג. הערה על דף קכב:

How to Excel in Learning

קידושין

קד. הערות על דף ב.
קה. (דף ב.) שווה פרוטה
קו. (דף ב.) הערות על ברכת דוד קידושין סימן א', בענין שוה כסף ככסף
קז. (דף ג.) ביאור מחלוקת בין רש"י לתוס רי"ד בקידושין ע"י חליפין
קח. (דף ה.) חופה קונה
קט. (דף ו.) המקדש במלווה
קי. הערות על דף ז.
קיא. הערות על דף יז:

נדרים

קיב. (דף ב.) התפסה
קיג. (דף ב.) ההבדל בין נדרים ובין חרמים
קיד. (דף ב.) עיקר הנדר
קטו. (דף ב:) בענין גדר של חפצא
קטז. (דף ב:) בענין ההבדל בין נדרים ושבועות
קיז. (דף ב:) ההבדל בין איסור חפצא ואיסור גברא
קיח. הערה על דף ד:
קיט. (דף ז.) ברכת שמואל בענין יש יד לצדקה
קכ. הערה על דף ט.
קכא. (דף יא.) תנאי כפול
קכב. הערה על דף יא:
קכג. הערה על דף יב.
קכד. עוד הערה על דף יב.
קכה. הערה על דף יב:
קכו. הערה על דף יג.
קכז. עוד הערה על דף יג.
קכח. הערה על דף יד.
קכט. (דף יד.) התפסה לפי הר"ן
קל. (דף טו.) בענין קונם עיני בשינה
קלא. (דף טז.) נדרים ושבועות לעבור על המצות
קלב. הערה על דף טז.
קלג. (דף כא.) ההבדל בין פתח וחרטה
קלד. (דף כב.) מתחרט על הנדר א"צ להתחרט על קיום המעשה
קלה. (דף כה:) נדרי שגגות
קלו. הערה על דף כה:

128

קלז. (דף כו:) גמר בלבו צריך להוציא בשפתיו
קלח. (דף כז.) אנוס רחמנא פטריה
קלט. הערה על דף כז:
קמ. (דף סד:) ההבדל בין נולד ושאר פתחין
קמא. הערה על דף סח.
קמב. (דף סח:) ההוא גינא
קמג. (דף סח:) הערה על דף סח:
קמד. (דף סח:) ביאר הר״ן ד״ה שמע בעלה וכו׳
קמה. (דף סט:) קיים ליכי ומופר ליכי
קמו. (דף עא.) האב לחודיה מיפר או האב והבעל מפירים ביחד
קמז. (דף עא:) "מיגז גייז"
קמח. הערה על דף עה:
קמט. (דף עט:) חזקה גבי סתם שתיקה
קנ. הערה על דף פב:
קנא. (דף פה:) "דאפקריה"
קנב. הערה על דף פו:
קנג. הערה על דף פז:
קנד. קצות החשן סימן רע״ג אות א׳

נזיר

קנה. אם נזירות בגדר נדרים או שבועות

גיטין

קנו. (דף ב:) הערה על תוס׳ ד״ה לפי שאין בקיאין
קנז. הערה על דף כז.
קנח. (דף לב:) הערה על תוס׳ ד״ה ורב נחמן
קנט. (דף לג:) עדות שבטלה מקצתה בטלה כולה
קס. הערה על דף נה:
קסא. הערה על דף סב:

129

How to Excel in Learning

קסב. הערה על דף סה.
קסג. הערה על דף עז.
קסד. (דף פב.) "אלא" "חוץ" או "ע"מ"

בבא קמא

קסה. (דף ב.) לא הרי
קסו. בענין מזיקין הנלמדין בצד השוה דף ג,ו
קסז. תולדה דרגל דף ג.
קסח. הערה על לא ראי הקרן דף ג:
קסט. הערה על דף ו:
קע. (דף ז.) בענין מיטב
קעא. כולן נכנסו תחת הבעלים דף ח.
קעב. אחים שחלקו דף ט.
קעג. רש"י ד"ה בחצי נזק צרורות דף ג
קעד. ברכת שמואל ב"ק סימן ט' אות ב'
קעה. סוגיא של זה נהנה וזה לא חסר דף כ.
קעו. (לו.) הערה על "יחזיר"

בבא מציעא

קעז. (דף ב.) ביאור על תוס' ד"ה ויחלוקו
קעח. (דף ב:) ביאור על תוס' ד"ה ומה וכו'
קעט. (דף נז:) בענין אם יש לקרא העדר אחריות נגד אבידה וגניבה בשומר שוכר בשם פשיעה
קפ. (דף ע:) הערה על פרק ה. משנה ו'
קפא. (דף עח.) תירוץ פרק ו' משנה ג'
קפב. (דף עח.) ביאור על תוס' ד"ה הוחמה (חידושי רבי ראובן ב"מ סימן כא)
קפג. (דף צג.) תחילתו בפשיעה וסופו באונס
קפד. (דף צג:) ביאור על תוס' ד"ה אי הכי
קפה. (דף ק.) המחליף פרה בחמור (רבי שמעון זצ"ל)

בבא בתרא

130

How to Excel in Learning

קפו. (דף ב.) ביאור על המשנה
קפז. (דף ב.) ביאור על תוס׳ ד"ה לפיכך
קפח. (דף ה.) בחזקת שנתן
קפט. הערה על דף כב:
קצ. (דף כג:) חזקת הבתים
קצא. (דף כט.) בענין חזקת שלש שנים
קצב. הערה על דף לא.
קצג. הערה על דף לא:
קצד. (דף לג:) לא חציף איניש
קצה. (דף לד:) ההוא ארבא
קצו. (דף לה:) ביאור על תוס׳ ד"ה ואי לפירא
קצז. הערה על דף פו:
קצח. הערות על דף צה:
קצט. הערה על דף צו:
ר. הערה על דף קג:
רא. (דף קיא:) פחות משתות, הגיעו; עד שתות, ינכה
רב. הערה על דף קיב.
רג. הערה על דף דף קעו:

סנהדרין

רד. (דף ד.) ביאור על רש"י ד"ה בחלב אמו
רה. (דף ה.) ביאור על רש"י ד"ה יוסיפו הדיינין
רו. (דף ה.) ביאור על רש"י ד"ה דן אפ׳ ביחיד
רז. הערה על דף יח:
רח. הערה על דף כג:
רט. ביאור על רש"י ד"ה שבשאר מצות שגג
רי. הערה על המשנה בדף עג.
ריא. הערה על דף עז:
ריב. הערה על דף עח.
ריג. הערה על דף קיב.

מכות

ריד. (דף ב.) הסבר על לשון "הא כיצד העדים נעשים זוממין"
רטו. (דף ב.) ביאור תוס׳ ד"ה מעידין

131

How to Excel in Learning

ריו. (דף ב.) תקפתא של רבינא
ריז. (דף ב:) הסבר על לשון "לאו בני כפרה נינהו"
ריח. (דף ד.) ביאור על תוס' ד"ה לוקין
ריט. (דף ד:) ביאור על תוס' ד"ה רבנן
רכ. (דף ה.) הפטור מהעונש של "כאשר זמם"

שבועות

רכא. (דף ו.) בענין נגעין
רכב. (דף כ.) בענין של איסר
רכג. הערה על דף כה.
רכד. הערה על דף כו.
רכה. (דף כו.) שגגתה בשבועה
רכו. (דף כח.) ביאר רש"י ד"ה אין איסור השבועה חל עליו וכו'
רכז. (דף ל:) כל מקום שיש חילול השם אין חולקין כבוד לרב
רכח. הערה על דף לא:
רכט. (דף לב.) צמצם ותוך כדי דיבור בענין כפרים בעדות
רל. (דף לז:) משביע עדי קרקע
רלא. (דף לז:) קרבן שבועה וקרבן גזלה
רלב. הערה על דף מ.
רלג. הערה על דף מ:
רלד. (דף מ.) ביאר תוס' ד"ה בטוענו
רלה. (דף מג:, מד:) מחלוקת ר"א ור"ע
רלו. הערה על דף מד:
רלז. עוד הערה על דף מד:

עבודה זרה

רלח. (דף סב.) איסור שכירות

132

How to Excel in Learning

<u>משניות</u>

רלט. דמאי פרק ו משנה ב
רמ. דמאי פרק ו משנה ח
רמא. חלה פרק ב משנה ו
רמב. נגעים פרק ד משנה ח
רמג. קינין פרק א משנה ג
רמד. קינין פרק ב משנה א
רמה. מנחות פרק ז משנה א

<u>עניני בר מצוה</u>

רמו. כוונת הלב במצות ספירת העומר
רמז. קטן שנתגדל בימי הספירה
רמח. בענין חיובים המוטלים על קטן ועל בחור בר מצוה
רמט. המידה של עזות
רנ. ברכת ברוך שפטרני
רנא. קטן ובחור בר מצוה וד' פרשיות

How to Excel in Learning

עמוד שלם בתחילת הספר

Front page dedication

/ להקדשה לרפואה /

/ לעילו נשמה להצלחה /

בסכום $15,000

עמוד שלם בסוף הספר

Back page dedication

/ להקדשה לרפואה להצלחה /

לעילו נשמה בסכום $1000

חצי עמוד בתחילת הספר

Half front page dedication

להקדשה/ לרפואה/ להצלחה/ לעילוי נשמה

בסכום $3000

חצי עמוד בסוף הספר

Half back page dedication

להקדשה/ לרפואה/ להצלחה/ לעילו נשמה בסכום של

$500

How to Excel in Learning

בסכום
$250

רבע עמוד בסוף הספר

להקדש לרפואה שלמה/

לעילוי נשמה ולהצלחה.

On the following pages are

dedications of those who

have dedicated pages for the

of publication the complete sefer

Emrei Chayil

How to Excel in Learning

בס"ד

*As a small token of my appreciation,
this page is dedicated*

to my dear friend, who chooses to remain anonymous,

Our acquaintanceship spans over thirty years.

In the past ten years he has assisted my fundraising efforts by providing me with rugged and reliable vehicles, often with custom fitted systems, always with lifetime guarantees; and never at a cost to me. That means he has been donating, on an annual basis, over two thousand dollars in products and services to

the

American Friends of Yeshiva Kesser Chaim

May HaKodesh Barachu grant him, together with his entire family,

much hatzlacha and bracha and may they only have nachas from their entire family!

Sincerely,

Rabbi Y. S. Basner

לע"נ

אבי מורי יוסף בן מרדכי אנטן ז"ל

נפטר י"ז תשרי תשע"ו

אמי מורתי ציפורה בת בנימין אנטן ע"ה

נפטרת ל' סיון תשע"ה

אחי אברהם חיים בן יוסף אנטן ז"ל

נפטר י"ד תמוז תשע"א

דויד בן זלמן פינק ז"ל

נפטר י"ד סיון תשנ"ב

ע"י משפחת אנטין

How to Excel in Learning

מוקדש

בהערכה רבה

לתלמיד חכם גדול מקרית ספר
החפץ בעילום שמו על תרומתו
להדפסת הספר

How to Excel in Learning

לכבוד הרב חיים מנדל שליט"א

העמוד של ישיבת תורת חיים ותורת אמת של מיאמי

ושל כל העיר מיאמי

במשך עשרות שנים ידיד יקר וקרוב שלי,

ולכל מי שפוגש אותו,

אשרי יולדתו ואשרי משפחתו וכל תלמידיו

איש שמשמח כל מי שמדיבר איתו.

זכיתי להיות חברותא שלו בתחילת לימודי בישיבת חפץ חיים

וכשפתחתי את הכולל לפני 20 שנים הוא קיבל אותי בשמחה ועזר לי בנדיבות לב

ועוזר לי בגיוס הכספים במיאמי

אני מבקש מהקב"ה שיברך אותו ורעיתו בברכה והצלחה ותהיה להם רק נחת מכל משפחתו הבנים והבנות, הנכדים והנכדות

How to Excel in Learning

מוקדש

לרב מרדכי פרנקל ורעיתו

מקיו גראדנס הילס

על תרומתם הנדיבה

ותמיכתם בישיבת כתר חיים

במשך 20 שנה

How to Excel in Learning

לזכות

ברכה נחמה גאלדע בת מרים נענא

רפואה שלימה

לחיים יהודה בן יענטא גיטל

How to Excel in Learning

Mazal Tov

to

Rabbi Basner

on the progress in the publication

of his seforim

Tzvi and Emily Schwartz

Baltimore, MD

How to Excel in Learning

מוקדש

לד"ר ג'ימס וורנוב

לזכות

ירחמיאל בן זושא

מוקדש ע"י יוסף דעטשער

לע"נ

אהרון יעקב בן שמואל

משה יחיאל בן נפתלי

How to Excel in Learning

In

Honor

of our

Wonderful Parents

Dr. Rene and Beloria Levy

and

Rabbi Ezra and Shifra Kanon

From

Dr. Eliyahu and Miriam Levy

of

Seattle, Washington

How to Excel in Learning

In memory of our parents

הרב יוחנן בן שמואל זאב

חי-ה טיובע בת זאב

Of the first Talmidim of

Hagaon R' Alter Henoch Leibowitz, Zatzal.

Marbetzei Torah

who served the Klal selflessly for many years

and who were zocheh to produce

generations of Bnei Torah.

ת.נ.צ.ב.ה

Rachel And Bentzion Chait

About the Author

Rabbi Yerachmiel Shlomo Basner learned in Yeshivas Rabbeinu Yisroel Meir HaCohen, Baal Chofetz Chaim z`tl (widely referred to as Yeshivas Chofetz Chaim), in Queens, New York and in Yerushalayim. After 18 years, he learned at Knesses Yehuda and other kollelim, and received Semicha from HaRav HaGaon Zalman Nechemya Goldberg, shlita. He has a Teacher's Certificate from Rabbi Hillel Mandel's Torah Educator's Institute, a Certificate from Ohr Lagolah Leadership Training Program, a Professional Coach Diploma Certificate from the Refuah Institute, and a Professional Coach Certificate from the American Association of Professional Coaches.

Rabbi Basner has lectured on Techniques for Optimizing Learning, and Memory Enhancement. In 5751, with the haskama of HaRav HaGaon Rabbi A. Henoch Leibowitz, zt`l, Rosh HaYeshiva of Chofetz Chaim, he started a kollel, The Institute for Talmudic Skills. He reorganized the kollel in 5757 under the name

How to Excel in Learning

Yismach Leiv Mercaz Torani Kiryat Sefer. In 5766 the name was changed to Yeshiva Kesser Chaim. From his exposure to different kollelim, Rabbi Basner has synthesized an approach to iyun that emphasizes the need for precision of thought about the point under discussion in the context of the entire sugya.

His approach to learning and teaching has consistently captivated his talmidim, penetrating language and cultural barriers, and inspiring both young teenage Israelis and mature baalei teshuva, as well as advanced English-speaking and Israeli avreichim.

Presently is working on publishing his shiurim and explanations from the last twenty five years. These includes sugyas on mathematics.

If you have felt that this guide has been helpful and you would like others to have a chance to read it, then please send your supportive comments to the author, either in writing or email. This can help publicize the guide.

Made in the USA
Columbia, SC
09 October 2024

44040741R00090